The Great Big Book of Classroom Songs, Rhymes and Cheers

200 Easy, Playful Language Experiences That Build Literacy and Community in Your Classroom

by Ellen Booth Church

with Deb Hensley

SCHOLASTIC
PROFESSIONAL BOOKS

New York ✳ **Toronto** ✳ **London** ✳ **Auckland**
Sydney ✳ **Mexico City** ✳ **New Delhi** ✳ **Hong Kong**

To Deb Hensley—whose professional and playful collaboration
made this book not only possible, but fun!

Acknowledgments

The publisher has made every effort to trace the ownership of all copyrighted material and to secure permission from copyright holders. • "A Bird Came Down" by Emily Dickinson is reprinted by permission of the publishers and the Trustees of Amherst College from *The Poems of Emily Dickinson*. Ralph W. Franklin ed., Cambridge, MA: The Belknap Press of Harvard University Press, copyright © 1998 by President and Fellows of Harvard College. Copyright © 1955, 1961, 1979 by President and Fellows of Harvard College. • "April Rain Song" from *Collected Poems by Langston Hughes*. Copyright © 1994 by the Estate of Langston Hughes. Reprinted by permission of Alfred A. Knopf, a division of Random House, Inc. • "Happy Birthday to You" by Mildred J. Hill and Patty S. Hill © 1935 (Renewed) Summy-Birchard Music, a division of Summy-Birchard Inc. All rights reserved. Used by permission. Warner Bros. Publications U.S., Miami, FL 33014.

Cover design by Jaime Lucero
Cover illustration by Anne Kennedy
Interior design by Lefty's Editorial Services
Interior illustration by James Hale
Edited by Karen Kellaher
Creating Your Own Rhymes With Children section written by Deb Hensley

ISBN: 0-590-37607-1

☆ Contents ☆

Introduction

Why Use Rhymes and Poems?

Preschoolers and young students find words, sounds, and rhythms delicious. Nonsense rhymes, funny words and sounds, repeating patterns and rhythms...mix them up and put them all together and you have poetry! And, as you'll discover as you use this book, poetry can be a teacher's best friend. It not only is a delightful language experience. It is also a perfect tool for exploring the curriculum areas and for headache-free classroom management.

Poetry Power

Even though rhymes and poems are very popular with children, many teachers are reluctant to use poetry in their classrooms. Are you? I once was. Maybe it was the "seriousness" many people equate with poetry, or perhaps it was childhood memories of memorizing poems to recite in front of the class! Fortunately, over the years I have realized that poetry is not only a luscious language activity but it actually is FUN. It is all in how you present it, and this book will help you do so in a way that's engaging and irresistible.

Poetry is an excellent way to introduce vocabulary and literacy skills. Because poems are often predictable and brief, kids can master them quickly. For many, a poem or nursery rhyme may be their first successful "reading" experience. Poems can be repeated often, so kids can quickly gain familiarity with them. Poems' rhythms make them easy to remember while poems' rhyming words make them accessible and predictable. Teaching with poems is different from the "old days," when children had to stand in front of the class and painfully recite a memorized poem. (I was one of those shy kids!) "Saying" a poem can be a group choral experience, to be shared and enjoyed by all.

Make Time for Rhymes

To make the most of the poems in this book, you might choose to introduce one poem a week. I called this event "Poem Monday." It was one way we made the start of the week special. Sometimes I shared a poem that related to our curriculum or to a favorite theme, but often the rhyme was just

something fun I had discovered. I started each Poem Monday by writing the day's poem in large letters on an experience chart so that all the children could see it. It did not matter that the children couldn't read the words; they were making important links between oral and written language.

To entice the children into the merriment, I used a fun question, riddle, prop, or puppet. Once students' enthusiasm was bubbling, I would "perform" the poem with the same dramatic elements I used when I read a book or told a story. (Nothing ruins a poem more than a flat, unpracticed reading!) After cries of "Do it again," I would repeat the poem, this time inviting children to add a rhyming word here or a line there. Soon our Mondays were filled with poem recapitulations. We'd share our poem together several times at group time plus a few additional times throughout the day.

Often, a treasured poem reappeared throughout the week. We'd play with the poem at group time, in the learning centers, at snack time, and outside! As you move through this collection, you'll likely find many of your own ways to bring the chants, poems, and rhymes alive.

Poem Monday
Today is Monday.
Today is Monday.
Monday is poems....
All the little children,
Come and eat them up!

The Flexibility of Poetry

In addition to setting aside a special time for rhymes, you should consider using rhymes, poems, and chants through the day and across the curriculum. Of course, one of the most important moments in any preschool or primary-grade day is meeting or circle time. You can use rhymes during this time to help all students feel part of the classroom community—and to get students to do what you need them to do (line up, sit, quiet down, etc.). You'll find additional tips on incorporating poems into circle time in chapter 1. Rhymes and poems also make great

additions to lessons in social studies, math, science, and language arts. (Even if you don't yet use these subject-area titles, you probably teach topics from these categories.) Launching a unit on weather? There are countless poems about rain, wind, sun, and snow to grab your students' attention; look for many of them in chapter 8 of this volume. Trying to introduce consonant or vowel sounds? Check out the dozens of alliterative ABC poems in chapter 6. The rhymes in this book can also help you teach about counting, animals, physical fitness, nutrition, telling time, the seasons, cultures from around the world, and much more. By using a poem to introduce or enrich a lesson, you not only set the mood perfectly, you also let students know that someone else was so fascinated with this topic, they wrote a poem about it!

Tips for Sharing Rhymes

The following are some tried-and-true techniques I have used to foster a love of rhymes and poetry in my own classroom. You'll find other suggestions following each poem in the collection.

* Whenever possible, add a hand or body motion to go with a rhyme or song. Children love movement, and even if they can't remember the words, they can at least perform the motion with you!

* Repetition, repetition! Preschool children love to say "Let's do it again!" Listen to them! Repetition is the key to the development of many important language skills.

* Before introducing a new rhyme or song, be sure to say some familiar favorites that children already feel successful with.

* Add props and puppets to help a poem come alive: flannel board, stuffed animals, story boxes, poem charts, etc. You can also try drawing "what's missing" pictures and have students guess the missing component (for example, show a cow jumping over an empty space).

* Make copies of favorite rhymes and send them home. Young children can rarely remember all of the words, and parents will appreciate the opportunity to read the poem to children at home. You can also make an audio or video tape of children singing or saying the rhymes for parents to borrow. They will be delighted to hear how it is supposed to sound and to see or hear their own children.

* Write it down! Even if your students can't read, they are still fascinated by letters and words. Using your best primary writing, print the rhymes on chart paper. Add rebus illustrations next to common words whenever possible for children to use as picture clues. Or, invite students to illustrate the poems themselves. Hang the rhymes on a flip chart so that children can revisit their favorites later.

* Wear a costume in order to inhabit the rhyme. Dress the part of one of the characters or wear something that will remind children of the rhyme. Then BE DRAMATIC!

* Use Pocket Charts for children to add or change words or rebus pictures for the poem.

* Tape record children saying the poem. Put the recording in the listening center with the poem and any corresponding props for independent recitations!

* Collect the "Monday Poems" in a class book for children to take home and cherish at the end of the year.

* Create poem "inventions" based on predictable repetitive poems and lyrics. (We turned "I Know an Old Lady Who Swallowed a Fly" into "I Know a Poor Pelican Who Swallowed a Pie." Amazingly, all he could eat were things that started with "p"!)

* Introduce picture books that are based on poems or song lyrics.

* Encourage children to choose a poem to illustrate in book form.

Circle Time or Meeting Rhymes

Most of us start our day by gathering children together for a group meeting, or "circle time." We gather in order to create a sense of community, to share our individual experiences and create exciting new ones. The practice of circle time reflects an ancient and universal tradition of gathering people in a circle to share stories, songs, rhymes, and friendship.

Why a Circle?

The circle is the shape of friendship,
It has no beginning and no end.
Everyone is heard and respected,
As an equal friend.
The circle holds us together,
No one is left out,
It creates strength and support,
And a safe place for "kids" to hang out!

You probably have discovered—as I have—that the joy of sharing a rhyme or song is multiplied by the number of people in the circle. The more friends who gather, the more magic that's created. Here are some rhymes and songs to add to *your* daily meeting time magic!

"To be a teacher in the right sense is to be a learner.
I am not a teacher... only a fellow student."
—Soren Kierkegaard

OFF TO KALAMAZOO

We are off to Kalamazoo.
(or any place you'd like: circle time, etc.)
Would you like to go there too?
All the way and back again.
You must follow our leader then.
You must follow our leader,
You must follow our leader,
All the way and back again.
You must follow our leader,
On our way to Kalamazoo!

☆Activities☆

Each day, put one student in charge of leading the class to circle time. As all the children join in the singing, the leader walks around the room, heading toward the circle. The leader can do special gestures or movements for the others to imitate as they follow: snap fingers, put hands on hips, put hands in the air, etc.

FOLLOW ME

Follow my Bangalory Man;
Follow my Bangalory Man;
I'll do all that I ever can
To follow my Bangalory Man.

We'll borrow a horse, and steal a gig,
And around the world we'll do a jig.
And I'll do all that I ever can
To follow my Bangalory Man.

☆Activities☆

As you sing this poem, try a new way to get the children to move from here to there: people patterns! As children get ready to go to circle time or some other activity, try lining them up in patterns according to gender (boy-girl-boy-girl), clothing color (red-blue-green-white, red-blue-green-white), or clothing styles (pants-pants-dress, pants-pants-dress). Invite children to help choose the pattern for the day.

LITTLE RED CABOOSE

Little red caboose, little red caboose,
Little red caboose behind the train. Toot, Toot!
Smoke stack on his back,
Going down the track,
Little red caboose behind the train.

☆Activities☆

* Start singing the song while you form a "train" of children on your way to circle time. Touch the children's shoulders when it's time for them to join the train. The fun part of this rhyme is that this time around, the honor is being last (the caboose) instead of first.

* Play "count the cars" just as you might with a real train. Once students are lined up and chugging their way to circle time, have the children count off with your help. When you are finished, ask: How many cars does our train have?

* Read *Freight Train* by Donald Crews, or other picture books featuring trains at story time.

FOLLOW ME

(Tune: *This Is the Way*)

Follow me to meeting time,
Meeting time, meeting time.
Follow me to meeting time,
We're going to have some fun.

Sing children's names in the song as they "hook" onto the train. For example:

Pedro now can join the train,
Join the train, join the train.
Pedro now can join the train.
We're going to meeting time.

Activities

* Here's another fun take on the train theme. With this rhyme, students will love hearing their names called aloud. Use the rhyme whenever you need to take your class to circle time, lunch, outdoors, etc.

* When children leave circle time, invite them to change the rhyme to feature a new type of vehicle. You might say, "Look!" All of a sudden we are surrounded by water. What vehicles do we need to be now?"

FOLLOW ME

(Tune: *Mary Had a Little Lamb*)

Follow me to circle time,
Circle time, circle time.
Follow me to circle time;
We're going to have some fun!

Surprise children by adding new movements each day:

Skip with me to circle time...
Crawl with me to circle time...
Hop with me to circle time...
Tip-toe with me to circle time...
Swim with me to circle time...
Quack with me to circle time...

☆Activities☆

* As you sing this song, create a "snake" line and collect children as you move through the room. When everyone has been gathered on the line, weave throughout the room. Move fast and slow, high and low, etc.—until you circle them down to sit for meeting!

* After you sing the rhyme once or twice for children, ask them if they recognize the tune (*Mary Had a Little Lamb*). If students are confused by the different words, encourage them to clap out the rhythm of the rhyme as you sing.

WE CAN JUMP!

We can jump, jump, jump.
We can hop, hop, hop.
We can clap, clap, clap.
We can stop, stop, stop.

We can shake our heads for "yes."
We can shake our heads for "no."
We can bend our knees a little bit,
And sit down slowly...

✩ Activities ✩

* Although children probably know how to shake their heads for "yes" and "no," it wouldn't hurt to demonstrate. Explain that shaking our heads is one way we can communicate without speaking. Have children think of other words or phrases we can convey with gestures and facial expressions (hello, good-bye, something stinks, hurrah, etc.).

* Rewrite the first verse using new rhymes for lines 2 and 4. For example: We can walk, walk, walk...We can talk, talk, talk.

* Use this rhyme when children have gathered in your circle time area but are still giddy from the morning's activities. The rhyme gives children a chance to use up some energy by hopping and clapping, then moves on to gentler, quieter activities. By the time you are through with the rhyme, you'll have all of your children sitting in place, ready to start circle time.

TWO LITTLE HANDS

Two little hands go clap, clap, clap.
Two little feet go tap, tap, tap.

Two little hands go thump, thump, thump.
Two little feet go jump, jump, jump.

One little body turns around and around,
And then sits quietly down.

 ## Activities

* Use this as a welcoming activity on days when children are especially active. It will give them an opportunity to use their energy in productive ways and, like the previous rhyme, has a defined, quiet ending!

* Encourage children to think of other sounds and motions their hands and feet can do in the chant. Experiment with both loud and soft sounds.

* Ask a divergent question: How many different ways can you move around and around? (Some examples: wiggle, crawl, tip-toe, side step.)

* Invite children to suggest more body parts to say in this chant. What could two little eyes or ears do? What could one little head do? Create new verses and write them down on an experience chart for future renditions.

I STAND ON TIP-TOE

I stand on tip-toe
To make myself tall.
I bend my knees
To make myself small.
Now I'm tall, now I'm small.
But now I like my sit-down size best of all!

☆ Activities ☆

* Young children enjoy exploring the span from big to small and back again. Any activity that invites them to experience this range is a favorite. Use this rhyme for getting children ready for circle time. Not only will they enjoy the movement, but they will feel a bit tired at the end!

* Explore the concept of opposites with this rhyme. Talk about tall and small as being opposite qualities of size. Brainstorm a list of other opposites: short-long; heavy-light; big-little; etc. Use these the next time you sing the song.

* Compare the sizes of different items with non-standard units of measurement. Use classroom materials such as blocks or books to measure both tall and small things (door, waste basket, teacher, children).

I LIKE THE WAY

(Tune: *The Wheels on the Bus*)

I like the way that (child's name) is sitting,
 (or listening, walking, cleaning)
And I like the way that (child's name) is sitting.
I like the way that (child's name) is sitting...
Now we're ready to start the story!
(or go outside, play a game, get our coats)

✫Activities✫

✳ Does this sound too simple to work? It isn't, because you can never underestimate the power of positive reinforcement with young children! When children hear someone else's name sung in the song, they automatically want to have their names sung, too! They will immediately do whatever you are singing about (sitting, listening, cleaning).

✳ Keep singing! Some children take longer to pay attention than others. Sing the song until everyone has joined in, even if you have to repeat the children you've already named. They won't mind a bit; in fact, you might even hear them say, "Sing me again, sing me again!"

IF YOU'RE READY AND YOU KNOW IT

(Tune: *If You're Happy and You Know It*)

If you're ready and you know it,
Sit right down.
If you're ready and you know it,
Sit right down.
If you're ready and you know it,
Your smile will really show it.
If you're ready and you know it,
Sit right down.

If you're ready and you know it,
Look at me.
If you're ready and you know it,
Look at me.
If you're ready and you know it,
Your smile will really show it.
If you're ready and you know it,
Look at me.

☆Activities☆

Use this rhyme to get student's attention for circle time. If two verses do not do the trick—or if you are simply having too much fun to stop—add additional verses: If you're ready and you know it, say "I'm here," If you're ready and you know it, give a wink, etc.

HELLO, HOW ARE YOU?

(Tune: *Skip to My Lou***)**

Hello, <u>(child's name)</u>, how are you?
Hello, <u>(2nd child's name)</u>, how are you?
Hello, <u>(3rd child's name)</u>, how are you?
We're so glad to see you!

Chorus:

Here, here...We're all here,
Here, here...We're all here,
Here, here...We're all here,
We're all here in pre-k! (or kindergarten or school)

Hello, <u>(4th child's name)</u>, how are you?
Hello, <u>(5th child's name)</u> how are you?
Hello, <u>(6th child's name)</u>, how are you?
We're so glad to see you!

Repeat as many times as necessary to welcome each child!

☆Activities☆

* Invite children to animate the song with you. As the leader, you can go around the circle and shake hands with each child as his or her name is sung. Other children can shake hands with a child next to them.

* Experiment with saying "hello" in different languages. Insert the new word into the song and sing the rest in English. Invite bilingual students to share some words for "hello" the other children may not know. Some examples for you to try include:

French:	*Bon jour*
Italian:	*Ciao (chow)*
Swahili:	*Jambo*
Hebrew:	*Shalom*
Chinese:	*Nee-how*

WHERE, OH, WHERE IS...?

(Tune: *Mulberry Bush*)

Where, oh, where is ___(child's name)___?
Is ___(child's name)___? Is ___(child's name)___?
Where, oh, where is ___(child's name)___?
Peek-a-boo,
I see you!

☆Activities☆

* Use this rhyme to take attendance each day. If a student is not at school, sing, "I'm sad to say, home today" instead of "Peek-a-boo, I see you."

* Let students join the song, one at a time. You start off the rhyme by singing and playing peek-a-boo with the child to your right. Then that child sings and plays peek-a-boo with the classmate to his right, and so on. When the group comes full circle back to you, allow the whole class to sing, "Where, oh, where is our teacher (or your name)?"

* To add some fun, use a paper plate glued to a tongue depressor or painter's stick as a mask. When you say, "Peek-a-boo, I see you," pull the mask away from your face and look directly at the student whose name you have just called.

WHO'S THAT KNOCKING AT MY DOOR?

Who's that knocking at my door?
Who's that knocking at my door?
Who's that knocking at my door?
It is __(child's first name)__   __(last name)__ !

☆ Activities ☆

* Encourage children to sing with you. You sing the first three lines, then invite each child to sing his or her name on the fourth line. Encourage children to use both their first and last names in this welcoming song. If they can't remember both names you can sing them for them. After repeated experiences with this song, they will remember both names easily and proudly.

* Invite children to act out the song with you. Children can hide behind a bookcase or a cardboard "door," then knock on it and pop out at the end of the verse!

MY CHEER!

(Tune: *Twinkle, Twinkle*)

__(child's name)__ , __(child's name)__ ,
He's so neat!
He loves __(favorite food)__
When he eats.
His hair is __(hair color)__
and __(hair length or style)__ , too.
He's my friend and
You can be too!

☆Activities☆

✳ This is like a cheerleading chant that children can create in their own honor! Sing about a few children to model the rhyme, inviting each child to pipe up with what they like to eat and what they look like. Later, have children create their own rhymes about themselves or a partner. Remember, the words in the blanks don't need to rhyme!

✳ Use this when you are celebrating the "Child of the Week." Say the child's cheer at the beginning of each circle time to welcome him or her. You can invite the child and others to suggest other verses. Write the cheer in big letters on a chart, leaving space for the child to illustrate. Children will return to the chart frequently during the week to "read" and say the rhyme. Send the child's rhyme home at the end of the week so that families can celebrate too!

I SPY, WHO AM I?

I spy with my little eye,
Someone who is wearing __(describe child's clothing)__
Who am I?

I spy with my little eye,
Someone who has __(describe child's hair)__
Who am I?

I spy with my little eye,
Someone who has __(describe child's eyes)__
Who am I?

☆Activities☆

* All young children love riddles, especially ones that deal with their favorite subjects...themselves! Play this game at meeting time for taking attendance, for developing listening and observation skills, and just for fun.

* After many experiences with the game, invite children to make up an "I Spy" rhyme for a friend in the class.

* Make an "I Spy" magnifying glass for use with the game. Draw a huge magnifying glass shape on two pieces of cardboard or oak tag. Cut a hole in the center of the shapes and attach clear plastic wrap between them to create the "glass." Children delight in using the glass when it is their turn to say the rhyme.

* Take the "I Spy" glass outside on a walk. Invite children to guess what you are looking at by the clues you give in the rhyme. Then let them take a turn!

THE SHADES GAME

Shades, shades,
This is me.
Tell me, tell me,
What you see!

⭐Activities⭐

* To play this rhyme game, one child puts on a pair of sunglasses and the class says the chant together. Then the children take turns describing something they see in the appearance of the child wearing the shades: red hair, blue jeans, a big smile, etc.

* Why not make your own sunglasses? You'll need some of those plastic rings used to hold soda six-packs together, glue, colored cellophane, and pipe cleaners. First cut apart the soda rings so that you have three pairs of glasses "frames." Then glue the cellophane onto the rims. Add pipe-cleaner ear pieces, and you'll have shades for everyone in your class.

COME TOGETHER

(Sing as a chant or to the tune of *Skip to My Lou*)

Come, come, come together,
Come, come, come together,
Come, come, come together,
Come together now.

Clap your hands together,
Clap your hands together,
Clap your hands together,
Clap together now!

Stomp your feet together,
Stomp your feet together,
Stomp your feet together,
Stomp together now!

Add other verses such as:

Spin, spin, spin around...
Tap, tap, tap your head...
Jump, jump, jump together...

End with:

Let's be still together,
Let's be still together,
Let's be still together,
Now sit quietly down.

☆Activities☆

* Use this song to gather children to circle time, and to give them an opportunity to use up some energy before they sit down. Vary the movements according to the needs and suggestions of the group.

* How can you make some song movements with a partner? Children can experiment with hand shakes, partner claps, even tickles!

SING A SONG OF CHILDREN
(Tune: *Sing a Song of Sixpence*)

Sing a song of children
As happy as can be,
Boys and girls together,
Playing happily.

Try to make a new friend
Each and every day,
And a million, billion, zillion smiles
Are sure to come your way!

☆Activities☆

* Use this song as a class "alma mater." To make the rhyme more specific to your class, you can change the word "children" to "pre-k" or "kindergarten." The song will be just as effective. Many classes use this as part of their morning ritual.

* Make rainbow streamers to help your kids sing a song of children! Put out a collection of different colored crepe-paper streamers. Children can cut off equal lengths of each color, fold the strips in half, and staple the folded end to keep it fastened. The next time they sing the song together, they can dance and shake their streamers as if they are doing a class cheer!

* Ask children to create their own lyrics specific to your class. Brainstorm some words to describe the class and write them on an experience chart (busy, noisy, silly, friendly, etc.). Next, brainstorm words for the things the children like to do (building, running, drawing, reading, etc.). Put them together to make a new first verse. For example: "Sing a song of children, As busy as can be; Boys and girls together, Reading happily!"

OVER THE RIVER

Over the river and through the wood,
To grandmother's house we go.
The horse knows the way
To carry the sleigh,
Through the bright and drifting snow.

Over the river and through the wood,
Oh, how the wind does blow!
It stings the toes
And bites the nose,
As over the ground we go.

Over the river and through the wood,
Now grandmother's hat I spy!
Hurrah for the fun!
Is the pudding done?
Hurrah for the pumpkin pie!

☆ Activities ☆

* Sing this traditional song at Thanksgiving time, when many students will be headed off to grandparents' or other relatives' homes for tasty feasts. Ask students how they travel to their Thanksgiving destinations: car, walking, airplane, bus, etc. Then change the line, "Over the river and through the wood," to match the students' travel plans. For example, you might sing: "Over the cities and through the air, to Aunt Cindy's house we go..."

* Make copies of this rhyme and send it home with students. Most adults know bits and pieces of the song, but not the whole thing. Students will be proud to share their newfound knowledge, and families might enjoy singing the song together.

THIS IS WHAT I CAN DO

This is what I can do.
See if you can do it too.
This is what I can do,
Now I pass it on to you!

 Activities

* This movement game is perfect for playing at circle time. Demonstrate the rhyme by chanting it while making a simple motion (such as spinning your hands, tapping your head, clapping to the rhythm of the rhyme). Then repeat the rhyme, encouraging all the children to join in the movement. At the end of the rhyme, pretend to pass the rhyme to the next child. He or she can create a new movement for everyone to try.

* The more movements you add, the more challenging this gets! After children are familiar with the chant and game, invite them to do it with larger movements while walking around the circle.

* Having a hard morning? Consider passing a warm smile, hearty handshake, pat on the back, or hug around the circle.

* Create "pass-along" pictures with crayons and paper. Here's how: Each child has a piece of paper and makes a few marks on it while the chant is being said. At the end of the rhyme, each child passes his or her paper to the child on his or her right. As the chant is said again, children add to the new pictures in front of them. The chanting, drawing, and picture-passing continues until the papers are back to their original owners!

TEN LITTLE FINGERS

I have ten little fingers
And they all belong to me.   *(Hold up both hands.)*
I can make them do things;
Would you like to see?

I can shut them up tight,   *(Close fingers into fists.)*
Or open them wide.   *(Spread hands apart.)*
I can put them together,   *(Clap hands together.)*
Or make them all hide.   *(Hide hands behind back.)*

I can make them jump high.   *(Wiggle hands over head.)*
I can make them go low.   *(Wiggle hands at sides.)*
I can fold them up quietly,   *(Fold hands together.)*
And hold them just so.   *(Fold hands in lap.)*

✩ Activities ✩

* Very young children love to imitate! Take advantage of this enthusiasm when you are trying to calm children down or get their attention. Just saying something like "touch your nose" will often bring children back to the activity at hand! A fun rhyme like this can work wonders!

* Create rhyming inventions by asking children to suggest other ways they can move their fingers. Then do the rhyme again with the new motions.

* Can you do the same thing with your ten toes? Toes are a lot harder to move than fingers, but I'll bet children can figure out some interesting ways to move them. Here's a silly example: "I have ten toes, and they belong to me. I can make them do things. Do you want to see? I can curl them up and put them out straight. I can hide them in a shoe or lay them on a plate!"

THE MORE WE GET TOGETHER
(Tune: *Did You Ever See a Lassie?*)

The more we get together, together, together,
The more we get together, the happier we'll be.
For your friends are my friends,
And my friends are your friends.
The more we get together, the happier we'll be!

☆Activities☆

* This classic song is a favorite for beginning or ending the day together. A celebration of friendship, it can be sung while sitting or standing in a circle, holding hands, and swaying side to side.

* Use the song as a circle dance! Walk together around the circle in one direction the first time through and return in the other direction when you repeat the song.

* Create a "class friends" mural. Children can draw self portraits and paste them on a giant oak tag circle to show the circle of friends in the class.

* Paint with your feet as you sing the song! Place plenty of craft or mural paper on the floor, and surround the paper with newspaper and a few wash buckets. Put out flat trays with paint-soaked paper towels (which act as stamp pads). Encourage children to step gingerly on the stamp pads with bare feet, then walk around the mural paper. Remind students to exit via the wash bucket. The resulting painting will definitely show the joy of getting together!

GOOD MORNING TO YOU

(Tune: *La Cucaracha*)

Good morning to you, good morning to you,
Time to get up, rise and shine.
Good morning to you, good morning to you,
Gee, you're looking mighty fine (cha, cha, cha!).

☆Activities☆

* Try using tunes and sounds from different cultures to widen the diversity of your rhymes. The words to this rhyme are simple, but the tune gives it a calypso beat. If you are unfamiliar with the tune, ask around your school or look for a CD or tape of Hispanic music at your local library.

* What other beat could you use with this simple good-morning song? A rap beat works great, as does a modified version of a gospel sound such as "Swing Low Sweet Chariot" or "When The Saints Go Marching In."

* Use rhythm instruments to enhance the song. Maracas and simple castanets are the perfect mood setters for this rhyme. Everyone can play along.

PLAYMATE

(Traditional Tune)

Say, say, oh, playmate,
Come out and play with me
And bring your dollars three.
Climb up my apple tree.
Crawl down my rain barrel.
Slide down my cellar door
And we'll be jolly friends,
Forever more!

☆Activities☆

* Don't know the tune? That's OK; just make one up! Try singing it up the scale, using one tone for each line as you sing your way to the top.

* Some of the activities in this song are based on ways of playing from long ago. Most children will not know what a rain barrel or cellar door is! Encourage children to update the tune by brainstorming the things they like to do with playmates. What would they like a playmate to bring along? What might they climb on or crawl down together? Add these details to the song.

* Traditionally, this is a clapping song. Encourage children to clap their hands together, slap their knees, and clap with a partner as you sing together.

* It is helpful for children to have play days with classmates outside school, particularly for children who have difficulty making friends in a large group. Make a copy of this song to send home to families along with the phone numbers and addresses of all the children in class. Encourage parents to ask their children whom they would like to play with.

WE ARE ALL TOGETHER

(Tune: *Did You Ever See a Lassie?*)

We are all together, together, together,
We are all together at circle time.

There's __(child 1)__ and __(child 2)__ ,
And __(child 3)__ , and __(child 4)__ .
We are all together
At circle time!

They go this way and that way;
And this way and that way.
We are all together
At circle time!

Repeat for all children in the class.

Activities

* When using this rhyme at circle time, have children whose names are called move around in a circle or make back-and-forth motions at their seats.
* Remember to do the original version of this song, too (See "Did You Ever See a Lassie?" on page 71). In fact, you might want to do the original first so that children can learn different ways to move during the last part of the rhyme.
* Use the song for calling attendance. As you sing the children's names, they can raise their hands and say "hello." Or create a photo attendance chart with children's snapshots. Have each child hang a cardboard tag on the chart next to his picture when his name is sung in the song.

THE LITTLE RED BOX SONG

(Traditional Tune)

Oh, I wish I had a little red box,   *(Use hands to shape a box.)*
To put my good friends in....
I'd take them out   *(Reach in box.)*
And XXX   *(Three pretend kisses on hands.)*
And put them back again.   *(Pretend to put friends back in box.)*

☆ Activities ☆

* Place an unbreakable mirror inside a red box (you can paint a shoe box red). Tell the children that a very special friend is inside the box and that they will each get a chance to look inside. Try the song again, using the box. Each child will discover that her special friend is herself!

* Encourage children to share a "friend" from home—a treasured stuffed animal, doll, etc. Each day a different child can be assigned to bring something in. Use the red box and the song to introduce the "visitor." The child places it in the box and takes it out to show the other children on the "kisses" part of the rhyme.

* Add verses featuring other gestures of friendship and love: Hugs, smiles, waves, winks, and handshakes can all be used in addition to kisses.

THIS IS THE WAY WE GO TO SCHOOL

(Tune: *The Mulberry Bush*)

This is the way we go to school,
Go to school, go to school.
This is the way we go to school,
So early in the morning.

    (child's name)   walks with mom or dad,
mom or dad, mom or dad.
    (same child's name)   walks with mom or dad,
So early in the morning.

    (child's name)   rides the yellow school bus,
the yellow school bus, the yellow school bus.
    (same child's name)   rides the yellow school bus,
So early in the morning.

    (child's name)   gets a ride to school,
A ride to school, a ride to school.
    (same child's name)   gets a ride to school,
So early in the morning.

Continue with as many different forms of transportation as are represented in your class.

⭐Activities⭐

* Help the children describe how they get to school. Then draw a very simple pie chart to show the class how many children in the class walk to school, ride the bus, ride a bike, ride in a car, etc.

* Make it a movement game! Tape to the floor a large sheet of mural paper on which you have drawn the "road" to the school. As others sing and sway to the song, one child at a time dances down the road to school and sits at that end.

I'M A NOISY MONSTER

By Ellen Booth Church

I'm a noisy monster, I live in a cave.
(Make cave with arms.)
I'm a noisy monster, I will not behave.
(Shake arms wildly and make faces.)
I'm a noisy monster, I jump up with the sun.
(Act out waking up.)
'Cause I can't wait to run outside and scare everyone!
(Make scary gestures and faces.)
I'm a noisy monster, I stomp and scream and moan.
(Stomp feet, scream ,and moan.)
I'm a noisy monster, I smash, crash, and groan.
(Do smashing movements with arms.)
I'm a noisy monster, and when the day is through,
(Act out sun going down.)
I crawl back in my cave and sleep, just like you!
(Crawl on floor and lay head on arms—pretend to sleep.)
Just like YOU!

Activities

* Having a noisy, crazy day? Transform it with a rhyme! Children often need a positive outlet for their "inner monster"—and this is the perfect solution. Invite children to act out and exaggerate the monster side of themselves; because the poem slows down at the end, you can even use it before rest time.

* Make monster puppets! Use an old sock for the head and an old necktie for a long, silly tongue. Glue (or carefully staple) the tie inside the opening of the sock so that children can roll the tongue up and stick it out whenever they want! Children can glue on collage materials such as yarn, buttons, paper, and fabric scraps to decorate.

SHOO FLY

(Traditional Tune)

Shoo fly, don't bother me.
Shoo fly, don't bother me.
Shoo fly, don't bother me.
I belong to somebody.

I feel, I feel, I feel like a morning star,
I feel, I feel, I feel like a morning star.

☆Activities☆

* At morning circle, sing this over and over again, inviting children to change the last verse to tell how they feel. Don't forget to tell how you feel today, too!

* Play the "Pass-A-Face" game. Sit children in a circle and make a face that expresses an emotion. You might say, "This is my happy (sad, scared, shy, silly) face. Now I'm going to take it off and pass it to the next person. You can put it on and show us your happy face. Then take it off and pass it to the next person. We'll keep passing our happy face until it gets back to me!" Pretend to put the face on, show the children, and then use your hands to pass it to the next person.

MY HAND SAYS HELLO

(Tune: *Farmer in the Dell*)

My hand says hello,   **(Waving)**
My hand says hello,
Every time I see my friends,
My hand says hello!

My eye says hello,   **(Winking)**
My eye says hello,
Every time I see my friends,
My eye says hello!

My smile says hello,   **(Smiling)**
My smile says hello,
Every time I see my friends,
My smile says hello!

Activities

* Encourage divergent thinking by inviting children to make up their own verses adding other ways to say hello with their bodies. Be prepared for children to think of some amazing and funny ways to say hello.

* Ask each child to demonstrate a hello movement for others to copy as they sing the verse together.

* At the end of the song, sing back over the verses suggested by children in reverse order, ending with a hushed chorus of, "My hand says hello." This is a great opportunity to foster listening and memory skills.

WHERE ARE MY FRIENDS?

(Tune: *Are You Sleeping?* or *Where Is Thumbkin?*)

Where are my friends?
Where are my friends?
Are you here?
Are you here?
Who has come to child care? *(or kindergarten or school)?*
Who has come to child care?
Tell me, please,
Tell me, please.

Where is ___(child's name)___?
Where is ___(child's name)___?
I am here!   *(Child answers.)*
I am here!   *(Child answers.)*
How are you today, ___(child's name)___?
I am well, thank you   *(Child answers.)*
Happy you're here.
happy you're here.

☆Activities☆

✳ Sing the song for each child. Even if some of the children are hesitant to sing their part, they will all love to hear their names sung in the song! You can invite stage-shy students to wave or smile as you sing with or for them.

✳ Use this song throughout the day with children. You could sing for a child who is engaged in the block area to get her attention or for all the children as you are inviting them to line up. Informal use during activity time allows children to learn the song well and react in their own creative ways.

WE'RE GLAD YOU'RE HERE TODAY

(Tune: *Farmer in the Dell*)

We're glad you're here today,
We're glad you're here today.
Give a cheer 'cause __(child's name)__ is here.
We're glad you're here today!

__(child's name)__ is here today,
__(child's name)__ is here today,
Have no fear 'cause __(child's name)__ is here!
__(child's name)__ is here today!

☆Activities☆

Suggest that each child shout out his name when his verse is sung. The other children can act as cheerleaders to make the honored child feel welcomed and special.

JACKANORY

I'll tell you a story of Jackanory,
And now my story's begun.
I'll tell you another of Jack and his brother,
And now my story's done.

☆Activities☆

✳ One of my grandmothers was a fantastic storyteller and would go on as long as we wanted, but if we asked the other one to tell us a story, she would simply say a Jackanory rhyme like the one above. It intrigued us even as it left us hanging! Use this rhyme to introduce storytime.

✳ With students' help, create a tale about Jack and his brother. Start the story with, "One day, Jack and his brother...," then turn to the student on your right to say the next line. Go around and around the circle until students are happy with their story's ending. You will probably need to step in after a while to make sure the tale reaches an ending at all!

CROSS-PATCH

Cross-Patch, draw the latch,
Sit by the fire and spin,
Take a cup and drink it up,
Then call your neighbors in.

☆Activities☆

* Did you know that "Cross-Patch" is a person? Ask: What does the rhyme tell Cross-Patch to do? Act out closing the door and doing some work, then pretend to have a drink of tea. Finally, pretend to open the door again and call in your friends.

* Discuss the meaning of the word "cross" (mad or angry). Ask the children to tell you things which make them cross. Then, have them make their very best cross faces.

* If you have a time-out system, use the rhyme to talk about the value of taking time out when you are feeling angry.

OPEN SHUT THEM

Open shut them.
Open shut them.
Give a great big clap!
Open shut them.
Open shut them.
Put them in your lap.
Creep them, creep them,
Creep them, creep them,
Right up to your chin.
Open up your little mouth but....
Do not let them in!

☆Activities☆

* Probably one of the most beloved of finger plays, this one is a great "back pocket" rhyme—something you can pull out of your back pocket when you need a way to get children's attention QUICKLY! Use it when settling in for circle time, lining up, waiting for lunch to arrive, or anytime you have some time to kill.

* Show students how to follow the very basic hand movements described in the rhyme: opening and closing the hands, clapping, etc.

* What if the singer of this song were a crocodile? How would we enact the song? Ask for a few volunteers to be the crocodile's jaws. Children can use their arms together to recreate the motion of the jaws opening and shutting. Then children can take turns creeping up closer and closer to the crocodile until it "opens up its BIG mouth....but" snaps closed while the creepers run away!

HAPPY BIRTHDAY TO YOU

Happy birthday to you!
Happy birthday to you!
Happy birthday dear ___(child's name)___!
Happy birthday to you!

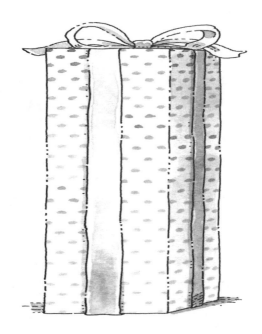

☆Activities☆

* Rhymes can help children remember special days from one year to the next. In my family, we sing this song in harmony and finish with a loud and enthusiastic flourish. Ask: What are your family traditions on birthdays?

* Some people use a second verse that asks, "How old are you now?" Others add silly verses like, "You look like a platypus, and you are one too!" You and your students can make up your own funny verses to this simple tune.

HOW MANY CANDLES?

How many candles?
Let me see.
Count them with me—
One, two, three   *(count to appropriate number)*.

Take a big breath
And blow them all out.
Your wish will come true,
But don't say it out loud!

☆Activities☆

✳ If you don't serve real birthday cake or cupcakes in your classroom, make a cardboard cake and put candles on it so that everyone can sing to the birthday girl or boy. Provide a "birthday badge" for the birthday child to wear all day.

✳ Consider having a "birthday book" program in your class. Instead of bringing in sugary treats for the party, the birthday child brings in a gift book for the class library. The book is read at the party. Later, place a label inside the front cover that marks the book as that child's birthday book gift to the class. This is a great way to extend your library while celebrating the joy of books!

POLLY'S BIRTHDAY

Polly had a birthday.
Polly had a cake. *(Make a circle with arms)*
Polly's mother made it. *(Make stirring motion.)*
Polly watched it bake.
Frosting on the top. *(Right hand held out, palm down)*
Frosting in between. *(Left hand moves under right palm)*
Oh, it was the nicest cake
That you have ever seen!
Polly had some candles,
One, two, three, four, five. *(Hold up fingers one at a time)*
Who can tell how many years
Polly's been alive?

☆ Activities ☆

* Challenge students to answer the math question posed at the end of the rhyme (Polly's been alive for five years). Ask: How many years have *you* been alive? How many candles did you blow out on your last birthday cake?

* Children love to think and talk about their favorite sweets. Invite students to illustrate a birthday cake they'd love to eat. Help them write descriptions of their cakes to go with the pictures.

GOOD-BYE FRIENDS

(Tune: *Good Night Ladies*)

Good-bye friends, good-bye friends,
Good-bye friends, we have to say so long.

Chorus:
Merrily we roll along, roll along, roll along.
Merrily we roll along as we go back home.

Sing the chorus again after each of these additional verses:

School is over, school is over,
School is over, it's time to end the day.

We'll be back tomorrow, we'll be back tomorrow,
We'll be back tomorrow, to start a brand-new day!

☆Activities☆

* It is important to end each day with a song or rhyme; it provides a feeling of peaceful closure for you and your students. Often, the end of the school day is a hectic time, and you may find that you have run out of time for your regular closing circle time. Don't despair! Use this song as a quick way to gather children for dismissal, even if you sing it together as children get their coats.

* If you do have time to share this at closing circle time, invite children to talk about something they did today that was really fun. Celebrate the day's accomplishments, and, if there were any bad moments, try to provide some perspective.

FRIENDS

(Tune: *Mulberry Bush*)

Friends I will play with you,
Sing with you,
Share with you,
And when every day is through,
I'll still be friends with you!

Friends, I might fight with you,
Cry with you,
Make up with you,
But when every day is through,
I'll still be friends with you!

☆Activities☆

✳ Use this at the end of a particularly difficult day. There is something reassuring about this rhyme. It allows children the right to get angry, to cry, and to make up, knowing that at the end of the day they will still have their friends' support. Children can suggest other words to describe the things that happen in class and add them to the song.

✳ Play a movement game using the first verse of this song. Help children form two circles, one inside the other. Sing the song and ask the circles to move around in opposite directions. (You may have to demonstrate or get an older child to help.) At the end of the verse, have children stop and turn to face each other (inside circle facing outside circle) and shake hands with their new friends. Sing the song again and again as children move around the circles and meet more and more new friends.

DEPARTURE TIME RHYME

Now it's time to say good-bye
To all our friends at play.
Some will walk and some will ride,
But we'll see them all (Day of the week you'll see children again) .

☆Activities☆

Say this rhyme together every afternoon as a wonderful way to teach children the days of the week. Be sure to hang a chart in your classroom that shows all the days of the week—with today circled or otherwise highlighted.

Movement Rhymes & Games

In order to fully comprehend things, young children love and need to use their whole selves. Moving their bodies and making sounds allows them to truly participate in any activity. Add some choice and an opportunity to cooperate and you have a recipe for great fun! You may find that children who are uncomfortable saying or singing a rhyme may feel more comfortable moving to it. From small hand movements, nods, and winks to fully embodied leaps and spins, children can use their bodies to say what they may not have words for. Be sure to create an environment of acceptance for children's attempts at moving. (HINT: Don't call it "dancing." For many children, that word is an immediate turn-off filled with images of perfect steps and frilly outfits.) When they know that there are no "wrong" ways to move, children will use their bodies to feel the creativity of childhood. So the next time you are saying a rhyme, invite children to create a new movement to "illustrate" it!

"Being still is how one clay clod sticks to another in sleep, while movement wakes us up and unlocks new blessings."
—Rumi

THERE WAS A LITTLE TURTLE

There was a little turtle.
He lived in a box.
He swam in a puddle.
He climbed on the rocks.
He snapped at a mosquito.
He snapped at a flea.
He snapped at a minnow.
He snapped at me.
He caught the mosquito.
He caught the flea.
He caught the minnow.
But he can't catch me!

☆Activities☆

* Children love this little rhyme on its own, but they'll have even more fun when you turn it into a game. You might start by asking, "Who wants to be a turtle?" and "Who wants to be a mosquito?" and so on until each child in the class is a turtle, minnow, flea, or mosquito. Then ask each group to think about the sound(s) their animals might make. After each group has decided on a sound mix, ask the children to close their eyes and find their fellow creatures by making their special sounds. Encourage them to listen carefully so they can find their group members. This is a great way to promote auditory discrimination. Of course they may not keep their eyes shut, but that's OK!

* When each group is re-united, chant the rhyme again. This time, have students keep the beat with drums or by clapping hands with a partner.

THE FARMER'S IN THE DEN

The farmer's in the den,
The farmer's in the den,
Eee-Aye-Eee-Aye,
The farmer's in the den.

The farmer wants a wife,
The farmer wants a wife,
Eee-Aye-Eee-Aye,
The farmer wants a wife.

Additional Verses:

The wife wants a child...
The child wants a sister (brother)...
The sister wants a grandmother...
And so on...

☆Activities☆

* This is a British version of the "Farmer in the Dell" that can include any family member the children would like to add. To play, have the children stand in a circle and hold hands. Choose one child to be the farmer; he or she will stand in the middle as the others sing and walk in a circle. When the group reaches the line, "The farmer wants a wife," the farmer chooses someone from the circle to step inside the ring with him/her. Feel free to change "wife" to "husband" if you'd like.

* To include everyone in the class, help students brainstorm other people who could be included in the rhyme: aunts, uncles, cousins, friends, teachers, etc.

REACH FOR THE CEILING

Reach for the ceiling,
Touch the floor.
Stand up again,
Let's do some more.

Touch your head.
Touch your knee
Up to your shoulders,
Like this, you see?

Reach for the ceiling.
Touch the floor.
That's all for now,
There is no more.

☆Activities☆

* This rhyme calls upon children to use large physical movements, such as bending down and reaching up. Use the rhyme to help your students use up excess energy in a positive way before they need to focus on quieter activities.

* Invite children to perform this rhyme as if they are horses, giraffes, or octopi. Ask: How does this animal move? How would it reach for the sky? How would it touch the ground?

* Another day, pretend to be trees or plants as you say the rhyme. First feel your roots in the ground, then your trunk or stem, and finally, your branches and leaves. Ask: How does it feel to be a tree?

I SENT A LETTER

I sent a letter to my love,
And on the way I dropped it.
A little puppy picked it up
And put it in his pocket.
It isn't you, it isn't you,
But it's you!

☆Activities☆

* Try this British nursery rhyme circle game. The children sit in a circle while one child walks around the outside of the circle. On "It's you!" he or she drops the letter behind a particular child. That child picks the letter up and races around in the opposite direction to get back to his place before the other child reaches it. Whoever is left out is "it" for the next round.

* Use a large manila envelope (or other envelope) as a prop to make the game seem authentic.

A TISKET, A TASKET

A tisket, a tasket,
A green and yellow basket.
I sent a letter to my love
And on the way I dropped it.
Someone must have picked it up
And put it in their pocket.

✫Activities✫

✳ This circle game is a lot like "I Sent a Letter," described on page 55. The children sit in a circle, except for one child, who runs or skips around the outside of the circle while the first three lines are being sung. When the rhyme reaches the line, "I dropped it...," the child drops the letter behind another child's back. The chosen child must get up and catch the letter deliverer before taking his own turn at delivering the letter.

✳ Set up a mailbox so that students can send each other cards and letters all year long. Discuss how the cards will be sorted and delivered.

OLD MACDONALD BUILT A HOUSE

(Tune: *Old MacDonald Had a Farm*)

Old MacDonald built a house,
E-I-E-I-O!
And on this house he put some walls,
E-I-E-I-O!
With a bang-bang here and a bang-bang there,
Here a bang, there a bang,
Everywhere a bang-bang.
Old MacDonald built a house,
E-I-E-I-O!

Old MacDonald built a house,
E-I-E-I-O!
And on this house he put some doors,
E-I-E-I-O!
With a bang-bang here and a bang-bang there,
Here a bang, there a bang,
Everywhere a bang-bang.
Old MacDonald built a house,
E-I-E-I-O!

☆Activities☆

* Children should act out the building of the house as the rhyme progresses, using play hammers or their hands to build the walls, etc.

* Add other verses to represent additional parts of the building: windows, a roof, stairs, bathrooms, a floor, etc.

GO IN AND OUT THE WINDOWS

Go in and out the windows,
Go in and out the windows,
Go in and out the windows,
As we have done before.

Stand and face your partner,
Stand and face your partner,
Stand and face your partner,
As we have done before.

Now follow her to Dallas,
Now follow her to Dallas,
Now follow her to Dallas,
As we have done before.

☆Activities☆

To enact this rhyme, children form a giant building by standing in a circle with arms outstretched. One child goes around the circle weaving in and out the "windows" (empty spaces between children) as the song is sung. At the end of the first verse, she or he chooses another child to be a partner while the second verse is being sung. During the third verse, the two children go through the building together on their way to Dallas or wherever they would like to go!

LONDON BRIDGE

London Bridge is falling down,
Falling down, falling down.
London bridge is falling down,
    My fair lady.

London Bridge has fallen down,
Fallen down, fallen down.
London Bridge has fallen down,
    My fair lady.

Build it up with iron bars,
Iron bars, iron bars.
Build it up with iron bars,
    My fair lady.

✧Activities✧

* This nursery rhyme can be sung and played as a movement game. Two children form an arch-like bridge with their arms, as a line of children go around and through the arch. At the end of the second verse the bridge falls down over one child to trap him. Then the child is released and the game continues as the bridge is fixed.

* Invite students to think of other ways they could "build up" the bridge in addition to iron bars.

GALLANT, GALLANT SHIP

Three times around went our gallant, gallant ship,
And three times around went she;
Three times around went our gallant, gallant ship,
'Til she sank to the bottom of the sea.

"Pull her up, pull her up," said the little sailor boy,
"Pull her up, pull her up," said he.
"Pull her up, pull her up," said the little sailor boy,
"Or she'll sink to the bottom of the sea."

☆Activities☆

❋ This nursery rhyme is played like "Ring Around the Rosie." To start, children dance around the circle holding hands. Everyone falls down at the last line of the first verse. Then, in the second verse, children pull each other up while still holding hands.

❋ Encourage students to count out "three times around" as they go in circles. It is a simple but enjoyable counting activity. You can also change the number of times the ship goes around to practice counting other numbers.

MY BIG BLUE BOAT

(Tune: *Wheels on the Bus*)

Oh, I like to ride on my big blue boat,
My big blue boat, my big blue boat;
I like to ride on my big blue boat.
Out on the deep blue sea.

My big blue boat has two red sails,
Two red sails, two red sails;
My big blue boat has two red sails,
Out on the deep blue sea.

My big blue boat has a place to sit,
A place to sit, a place to sit;
My big blue boat has a place to sit,
Out on the deep blue sea.

Additional Verses:

My big blue boat goes over the waves...
My big blue boat goes far away...
My big blue boat comes home again...

☆Activities☆

* This song is sung with partners. Children sit cross-legged in front of each other, hold hands and rock back and forth as they "row."

* Children can add verses telling about the parts of the boat, who is riding on it, and where it goes.

BIKE RIDE

(Tune: *Row, Row, Row Your Boat*)

Pedal, pedal, pedal your bike
Carefully down the street.
Round and round and round it goes,
Pedal with your feet!

☆Activities☆

* Have children make a pedaling motion with their legs while sitting in chairs or lying on their backs. This is great fun and great exercise!

* Together, rewrite the rhyme using different vehicles: drive your bus, steer the car, roll your skates, walk your feet, etc.

TEN TALL FIREFIGHTERS

Ten tall firefighters sleeping in a row.
"Ding," goes the bell and down the pole they go.
They jump into their fire trucks with no delay.
The sirens warn everyone to get out of the way.

With water from the big hoses they put the fire out,
"Hurrah, hurrah, brave firefighters!" all the people shout.
Then back to the station go ten tired firefighters,
To sleep until the bell wakes them up again.

☆Activities☆

Have students use their hands to act out the rhyme. To start, have students lay their hands flat on the table or desk. When the bell rings, the hands pop up, then make a steering motion as if driving to the fire. In verse 2, students pretend they are aiming a hose, then clap as the crowd cheers. Finally, students "drive" back to the station and lay their hands flat once again.

DOWN BY THE RIVER

Down by the river in an itty bitty pool,
Swam three little fishies and a mama fishie too.
"Swim," said the mama fishie. "Swim if you can."
And they swam and they swam right over the dam.

Boom, boom, didum, dadum, wadum, chew,
Ba, ba, ba, boom, boom, didum, dadum, wadum, chew,
Boom, boom, didum, dadum, wadum, chew,
And they swam and they swam right over the dam. SPLASH!

☆Activities☆

* Explain the meaning of the word "dam" to children in advance in order
  to avoid a serious case of the giggles. Demonstrate the concept by
  showing how the walls of the sink keep water from flowing out onto the
  floor.

* Have children do a swimming motion with their arms while reciting the
  first verse. Have them do claps, snaps, and foot stomps to keep the
  beat in the second verse.

WE'RE GOING TO MEXICO

We're goin' to Mexico,
We're goin' to the fair.
To see a senorita,
With flowers in her hair.
Oh, shake it, shake it, shake it,
Shake it if you can;
Shake it like a milkshake
And shake it once again.

Oh, rumble to the bottom
And rumble to the top,
And turn around and turn around,
Until you cannot stop!

☆ Activities ☆

To play this circle game, one child is the *senorita* or *senor* and stands in the center of the circle. Everyone else dances around the circle. During the "shake it" part, the child in the center dances alone, and on the "rumble" part, everyone shakes up and down. In the end the *senorita* or *senor* spins around with eyes closed and one arm pointing out. On hearing the word "stop," he or she stops and points to the next child to go in the center.

THIS LITTLE PIGGY

This little piggy went to market,
And this little piggy stayed at home.
This little piggy had roast beef,
But this little piggy had none.
And this little piggy went wee, wee, wee,
I can't find my way home (or "all the way home").

☆Activities☆

* This is a fabulous finger (or toe) rhyme which even very young children can appreciate. Take the child's thumb while saying the first line, then move across the hand touching a new finger as you say each subsequent line. When you reach the last line, run your finger up the child's arm and tickle him or her. Some children hate to be tickled even very lightly, so be sure to ask for permission first.

* Another exciting way to enjoy the rhyme is to invite five children to act it out. Each little "piggy" says his or her own line and acts out the corresponding action: shopping, sitting at home, eating, etc.

ROUND AND ROUND THE GARDEN

Round and round the garden
Walked a teddy bear.
One step,
Two step,
And tickle you under there!

☆Activities☆

* Take the child's hand and run your finger round and round the palm as you say the first two lines. When you reach the third and fourth lines, make two "steps" up the child's arm and gently tickle him or her.

* This is a "do it again" rhyme. Invent many different ways to make the teddy bear move. Can he skip? slide? hop? Have fun!

ENGINE, ENGINE NUMBER NINE

Engine, engine number nine
Running along the Chicago line;
Engine, engine number nine,
When she's polished she will shine!

✩Activities✩

✳ Start this rhyme by "chugging" around the classroom pretending you are a train. Invite one or two children at a time to join the train until everyone joins in. This can be a good chant to use to "inspect" the classroom after clean-up time to see if everything is put away and straightened up.

✳ Explain that a "line" (like the Chicago line) is the path a train takes. Then help children set up chairs or an obstacle course in a path around the room. Chant the rhyme again as your train follows the "Chicago Line" you have created together!

COCK, BULL, MAID, DUCK

(Letters Indicate Notes)

A: The cock's on the housetop blowing his horn;

C: The bull's in the barn a'threshing of corn;

E: The maids in the meadow are making of hay;

G: The ducks in the rain are swimming away.

☆Activities☆

Before you teach this rhyme to children, go around the circle and whisper one of the following words in each child's ear: cock, bull, maid or duck. Then ask children to listen for the word you whispered to them as you sing or chant this rhyme. You can sing it as an arpeggio if you like. When children hear their word ask them to pantomime what the rhyme says they are doing. You may need to help children identify movements for how to "make hay" and how to "thresh corn," especially if they are city kids!

LITTLE JUMPING JOAN

Here I am, little Jumping Joan;
When nobody's with me,
I'm always alone.

☆Activities☆

* This is a sweet little rhyme which can be easily extended into a movement activity. Simply ask children to do the same movement as Joan (in this case, jumping). Substitute a different movement each time you say the rhyme, and ask students for ideas. For instance:

  > *Here I am, little skipping Joan,*
  > *When nobody's with me*
  > *I'm always alone.*

  Other ideas include "creeping like a cat Joan," and "smiling Joan."

* Extend the activity by talking with children about what it feels like to be alone. Chart the feelings children have when they are alone: peaceful, scared, bored, miss my mom, etc.

DID YOU EVER SEE A LASSIE?

Did you ever see a lassie, a lassie, a lassie?
Did you ever see a lassie go this way and that?
Go this way and that way, and this way and that way,
Did you ever see a lassie go this way and that?

☆Activities☆

✳ Model actions for students to follow as you recite this familiar rhyme. Start by doing a simple back-and-forth movement with your head as you sing, then try a new movement.

✳ Make the activity a little more challenging by asking children to find a partner and make up a movement they can do together. Have each group share their movement with the larger group as you sing. This is a great way to teach cooperation and sharing of ideas.

TOMMY THUMB

Tommy Thumb, Tommy Thumb,
Where are you?
Here I am, here I am.   *(Hold up thumb)*
How do you do?   *(Move thumb up and down, as if bowing)*

Polly Pointer, Polly Pointer,
Where are you?
Here I am, here I am.   *(Hold up index finger)*
How do you do?   *(Move index finger up and down)*

Continue with Other Fingers:

Timmy Tall, Timmy Tall...   *(middle finger)*
Ruby Ring, Ruby Ring...   *(ring finger)*
Baby Small, Baby Small...   *(pinkie finger)*

Fingers all, fingers all,
Where are you?
Here we are, here we are,   *(Hold up all fingers)*
How do you do?   *(Move fingers up and down, as if waving)*

Activities

* Have children make hand prints in which each finger is a different color
  to match the rhyme. Ask students to predict how many colors they will
  need for their whole hand. When the prints are finished, you may wish to
  have students draw faces, hats, etc. on the fingers to represent the personalities introduced in the rhyme.

* Action rhymes like this one can sometimes be tricky for little children.
  Move slowly and repeat the rhyme frequently. By watching the youngsters try to learn the rhyme, you can gain useful information about their
  fine motor control.

HERE WE GO LOOBY LOO

Chorus:

Here we go Looby Loo
Here we go Looby Light
Here we go Looby Loo
All on a Saturday night.

Verses:

1. You put your right hand in,
You put your right hand out.
Shake it a little, a little,
And turn yourself about.

2. You put your left hand in...

3. You put your right leg in...

4. You put your left leg in...

5. You put your whole self in...

✫Activities✫

✳ When you chant or sing this rhyme, get everyone into a circle, join hands, and skip around for the chorus. For the verses, put the appropriate body part into the circle and shake it about.

✳ Games like this one are a terrific way to teach children the concepts of right and left. Dance to the rhyme frequently, and continue using the words "right" and "left" throughout your daily routine. For example, when you are helping a child put on his or her shoes, say, "Let's do the left one first today!"

Traditional Nursery Rhymes

Traditional nursery rhymes are a wonderful way to play with words and rhythm. These rhymes enjoy a special place in our culture and in our memories. Ask any adult to recite one, and they will probably do so with relative ease—even if they have not heard a nursery rhyme in many years. Nursery rhymes are embedded in our consciousness because they are often our first introduction to the rhythmic use of words and our beginning experience with literature.

What is the charm of nursery rhymes that has made them a staple in most children's early poetic diet? Perhaps it's the combination of rhythm and whimsy that delights the ear. Children often learn a nursery rhyme long before they know (or care to know) what it is about. They simply love the sound of the words, the repetition, and the beat. And that is how youngsters remember the rhymes. Even if a child can't recall a nursery rhyme's words, he can almost always clap to the rhythm or beat. For teachers and parents, the message is clear: Don't worry too much about a nursery rhyme's content. Discuss the content if it feels appropriate or try inventing new verses, but don't struggle to make the rhymes make sense!

Another wonderful aspect of nursery rhymes is that they demand participation. Listeners can't sit still; they must clap, shake, or act along to the words. Provide many opportunities for children to be part of the rhyme, both as individuals and a group. To encourage personal explorations, provide tape recordings and props or flannel board pieces for these rhymes in your learning centers. Add art materials so that students can create illustrations and puppets. Remember, nursery rhymes may seem old-fashioned to adults, but they are brand-new to every child who hears them!

**"It is the supreme art of the teacher to awaken joy
in creative expression and knowledge."
—Albert Einstein**

HUMPTY DUMPTY

Humpty Dumpty sat on a wall
Humpty Dumpty had a great fall.
All the King's horses
And all the King's men
Could not put Humpty together again.

☆Activities☆

✳ Act out this rhyme! Have the children move around the room like horses and soldiers. Assign one child to be Humpty, and have the others try to mend Humpty after his "fall." What would the King's horses and the King's men do to try to put Humpty together again? How would they all look and act when they could not put him together again?

✳ Humpty is usually pictured in illustrations as an egg, a very breakable item. Talk to the children about other things that are easily broken. What should they do if something breaks in the classroom? Work out a safety procedure with the children and make a poster for the wall. What can be fixed? What can't? Use the children's suggestions to make a display of things which are easy to break and tough to break.

✳ To help students master the art of "putting something together again," do jigsaw puzzles together. Discuss the strategies that one can use to assemble the puzzle: Find the edge pieces, match colors, match shapes. If you feel adventurous, you can even make a puzzle of your own. Paint a picture on paper, glue it onto thick cardboard, and cut it into a few irregular pieces.

CURLY LOCKS

Curly Locks, Curly Locks,
Will you be mine?
You will not wash dishes
Nor yet feed the swine;
But sit on a cushion
And sew a silk seam
And eat finest strawberries,
Sugar, and cream.

☆Activities☆

* This nursery rhyme is about living an easy, elegant life—with no chores and only the finest foods. Ask children to share their own ideas about how they'd like to be spoiled. Then talk about whether it's good to be spoiled.

* Ask: What chores do you help out with at home? Do you help wash the dishes? Set the table for dinner? Make your bed? Create a colorful graph to showcase students' responses.

SING A SONG OF SIXPENCE

Sing a song of sixpence,
      A pocket full of rye;
Four and twenty blackbirds,
      Baked in a pie.

When the pie was opened,
      The birds began to sing:
Wasn't that a dainty dish,
      To set before the king?

The king was in his counting house,
      Counting out his money;
The queen was in the parlor,
      Eating bread and honey.

The maid was in the garden,
      Hanging out the clothes,
When down came a blackbird
      And kissed her on the nose!

☆ Activities ☆

* This is a wonderfully busy rhyme to act out! Hats and other costumes can be used to identify the different characters, while props such as coins, clothesline, and a pie plate add depth to the enactment. Invite children to take turns pantomiming the characters while the others say or sing the rhyme!

* After you sing the rhyme "straight" start switching and mixing up the words. For example:
    Sing a song of sixpence, a pocket full of "pie"
    Four and twenty blackbirds, baked in the "rye"
    When the rye was opened, the birds began to "king"
    Wasn't that a dainty dish to set before the "sing"!

We promise there will be gales of laughter on the mixed up lines.

LITTLE MISS MUFFET

Little Miss Muffet
Sat on a tuffet,
Eating her curds and whey;
Along came a spider,
And sat down beside her,
And frightened Miss Muffet away.

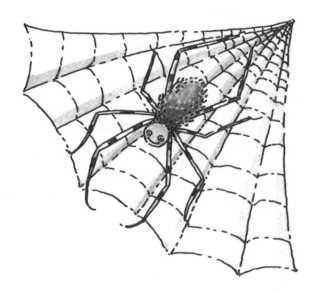

☆Activities☆

* Children can use this rhyme as a fingerplay much like "The Itsy Bitsy Spider." One hand can be Miss Muffet and the other the spider!

* When you mention spiders in your classroom, you'll probably be greeted with cries of "yuck" and "gross." Although many people are scared of spiders, these creatures actually help humans by eating insects. Without spiders, there would be many, many more bugs! Use this opportunity to talk about children's feelings about spiders and take a walk outside to observe them in nature. Children are usually fascinated by spiders' webs and can learn to keep a respectful distance from them (for the spiders' sakes).

LITTLE BOY BLUE

Little Boy Blue,
Come blow up your horn!
The sheep's in the meadow,
The cow's in the corn.
But where's the boy who looks after the sheep?
He's under the haystack, fast asleep!

☆Activities☆

* Invite children to be sheep and cows running around eating corn and misbehaving, while one child (wearing something blue!) pretends to sleep. Provide toy horns or make pretend horn sounds to wake him and collect the stray animals. Be sure that the "animals" know that they come back to the haystack when they hear the horn sound!

* What other colors could be used in the rhyme? Ask children to make up a new rhyme about "Little Girl Green." Brainstorm what she does and what happens in the rhyme. Try to use the rhythm of the original to guide you but don't worry about rhyming. Make it fun!

MARY, MARY QUITE CONTRARY

Mary, Mary, quite contrary,
How does your garden grow?
With silver bells and cockle-shells,
And pretty maids all in a row.

☆Activities☆

* Put toys or manipulatives in rows so that students get a mental image
  of what Mary's garden looks like. Still working in rows, start a pattern
  and invite students to uncover it and finish it for you. For example: purple flower, red flower, purple flower, red flower... You can also line students up and create a human pattern based on gender, shirt color, etc.

* Explain to students that silver bells and cockle shells are actually the
  names of flowers. Then invite children to draw what they think these
  flowers look like as part of a mural of Mary's garden. Children can also
  paste collage materials to create other flower varieties in the garden.

DIDDLE DIDDLE DUMPLING, MY SON JOHN

Diddle diddle dumpling, my son John
Went to bed with his trousers on;
One shoe off and one shoe on,
Diddle diddle dumpling, my son John.

✫Activities✫

* When you are talking to the children about the events in their daily routine, tell the children this rhyme so that they can have some fun. What is wrong with going to bed with your trousers on? What should John have done?

* Make up additional humorous rhymes about John. For example:

  Diddle diddle dumpling, my son John
  Went to school with his swimsuit on;
  One flipper off and one flipper on,
  Diddle diddle dumpling, my son John.

JACK SPRAT

Jack Sprat could eat no fat,
His wife could eat no lean;
And so between them both,
They licked the platter clean!

☆Activities☆

✳ Teaching nursery rhymes to young children helps them establish rhythm and learn to follow a steady beat. It also introduces new vocabulary within context so youngsters can begin to make some sense of new words. This rhyme is a good one to recite right before meal time or snack time. Talk about "fat" and "lean" foods and ask children if they know what these words mean.

✳ Play with the rhyme by reciting it in different ways. For example, have students recite the rhyme as loudly as they can, then as softly as they can. Or, have half the children say the first two lines and the other half the last two lines (the call and response method). This is great practice in listening and following directions.

JACK BE NIMBLE

Jack be nimble,
Jack be quick,
Jack jump over the candlestick.

☆Activities☆

* Such a simple rhyme and so much fun, this traditional nursery rhyme begs to be acted out over and over again. Use a stack of blocks to represent the candlestick and invite children to take turns jumping over it. Then add another block to raise the height of the candlestick and the excitement. After each group has cleared a height, raise it by one more block. How many blocks will the group be able to jump over?

* What other ways can Jack move? Brainstorm a list of movement words with the group and add these to the rhyme. For example, one new variation could be:

> *Jack be nimble,*
> *Jack be quick,*
> *Jack swim over the candlestick!*

JACK AND JILL

Jack and Jill went up the hill,
To fetch a pail of water.
Jack fell down and broke his crown,
And Jill came tumbling after.

☆Activities☆

* This is a perfect rhyme to use on tumbling mats. Use them combined with some sloped mats to create a very small hill for children to go up and tumble down. This is definitely a "Let's do it again!" activity children will love. If your students do not already know how, this is an excellent way to teach them to do somersaults.

* Add a little science to your day by asking students to think about what might have happened to the pail of water when Jack and Jill fell down the hill. Where did the water go? Go outside to the playground and experiment with dumping plastic pails of water down the slide!

I'M A LITTLE TEAPOT

I'm a little teapot,
short and stout.
Here is my handle,
Here is my spout.
When I get all steamed up,
Hear me shout.
Just tip me over and pour me out!

☆Activities☆

* This is a classic rhyme that almost every child loves, even if they don't know what tea is! Bring in an unbreakable teapot to show children. Examine the parts of the teapot that are in the song. Then serve iced herbal or decaffeinated tea for snack!

* Don't forget to set out the makings for a tea party in the dramatic play corner. Children can make "invitations" for each other and the classroom dolls and stuffed animals.

* This same tune can be used with another favorite food: popcorn! Try singing this rhyme to the teapot tune, then make popcorn to go with the tea for snack!

    I'm a little popcorn in a pot.
    Heat me up and watch me pop.
    When I get all fat and white I'm done.

MARY HAD A LITTLE LAMB

Mary had a little lamb,
Little lamb, little lamb.
Mary had a little lamb,
Whose fleece was white as snow.

And everywhere that Mary went,
Mary went, Mary went,
And everywhere that Mary went,
The lamb was sure to go.

It followed her to school one day,
School one day, school one day.
It followed her to school one day,
Which was against the rule.

It made the children laugh and play,
Laugh and play, laugh and play,
It made the children laugh and play,
To see a lamb at school.

✩Activities✩

✱ Discuss: What interesting pets have come to visit (or stay in) our classroom?

✱ Ask: What would happen if Mary brought her pet octopus for show-and-tell one day? How would the rhyme be different? Invite children to go through a list of funny and unusual pets that Mary could bring to school and discuss the consequences. Be absurd and silly with the ideas!

✱ Have a pet day in school! Ask children to bring in photos of their pets (or the pets they'd like to have) to share and discuss. Set up a pet display on a classroom bulletin board so that children can show off their pets all day!

BAA, BAA, BLACK SHEEP

Baa, baa, black sheep,
Have you any wool?
Yes, sir... yes sir,
Three bags full.

One for my mister,
And one for my dame,
And one for the little girl
Who lives down the lane.

Baa, baa, black sheep,
Have you any wool?
Yes, sir...yes sir,
Three bags full.

☆Activities☆

* Most young children do not know that wool comes from the coat of a sheep. If possible, bring in some examples of raw wool and wool yarn or fabric for children to feel and explore. It is important for children to know that the sheep is NOT killed in order to get the wool.

* The dramatization of this nursery rhyme provides a wonderful opportunity to practice one-to-one correspondence skills with the number three. Stuff pillowcases to represent the bags of wool. Create hats or masks to represent the other characters in the rhyme (sheep, mister, dame and little girl). When the rhyme is said, the black sheep hands one bag to each of the other characters. Eventually, use your imaginations to add more characters! Ask children to name others the sheep might give the wool to and add them to the rhyme. Challenge students with math questions as you go along. For example, ask: If we add two more characters, how many bags of wool do we need altogether?

THE CAT AND THE FIDDLE

Hey, diddle, diddle!
The cat and the fiddle,
The cow jumped over the moon;
The little dog laughed
To see such sport,
And the dish ran away
With the spoon.

☆Activities☆

* This rhyme is an example of pure whimsy that touches the fantasy world of the child's mind. Possibilities for conversation are endless: How did the cat and fiddle get on the moon? How did the cow get over it? How can a dish and spoon run? Talk with children about these wonderful images and listen to their interpretations.

* Ask children to consider: What happened next? Where did the cow land? Where did the dish and spoon go?

* Put on some recorded "fiddle" music for children to move and dance to in a re-creation of the fun. It will be sure to inspire smiles and laughter!

RUB-A-DUB-DUB

Rub-a-dub-dub,
Three men in a tub,
And who do you think they be?
The butcher, the baker,
The candlestick maker;
Turn 'em out, knaves all three!

☆Activities☆

✳ Ask children to use blocks to create a giant "tub" in the center of your circle time area. Then act out the rhyme over and over until all of the children have had at least one turn in the tub.

✳ This rhyme is a wonderful way to launch a discussion of the jobs people hold in your community. Although the rhyme is an old one, people today still work as butchers, bakers, and candlestick makers. But they have a wide variety of other careers, too. Invite children to make a list of the jobs they can think of. Ask them to consider which jobs they'd most like to try.

THERE WAS AN OLD WOMAN

There was an old woman
    who lived in a shoe;
She had so many children,
    she didn't know what to do.
She gave them some broth
    with honey and bread;
Then kissed them all sweetly
    and put them to bed.

☆Activities☆

∗ Use open-ended questions to get a discussion started about the rhyme: What would it feel like to live in a shoe? What would the inside look like? In this rhyme, is the shoe big or the woman little? Why do you think so?

∗ Serve honey and bread for snack time, then act out the singing rhyme "Roll Over" found on page 169 of this book. Invite children to pretend they are the "many children" all squeezed in bed as they sing and act out the song!

BANBURY CROSS

Ride a cock-horse to Banbury Cross,
To see a fine lady upon a white horse.
Rings on her fingers,
And bells on her toes,
She shall have music
Wherever she goes.

☆Activities☆

* Get out all your bells, triangles, jingle sticks and bands for an enactment of the fine lady on her white horse. Invite some children to clap the
rhythm of the rhyme while the other children adorn themselves with the
bells and other ringing instruments and gallop around the room. Say
the rhyme repeatedly so that the rhythm becomes natural AND the children get a good long ride! Switch groups and chant the rhyme again.
You can change the word "lady" to "laddie" if the boys object!

* Ask: What kinds of music do you think the fine lady likes to make?
Encourage children to suggest favorite songs to sing accompanied by the
bells and other instruments.

Multicultural Rhymes

You can travel the world in a rhyme. Without leaving your seat, you are whisked off to the sights and sounds of another land. Isn't poetry magical? Perhaps through this power of poetry the distance and differences separating cultures are transcended and the true connection of all humans can be experienced.

Here is a collection of rhymes from around the world. Although not every country is represented, these poems make an excellent starting point for exploration with young children. As children experience the sounds of various cultures, they will be eager to hear more. Your local library may offer additional collections of international poems and high-quality recordings of international songs. One good resource is *This Same Sky: A Collection of Poems from Around the World* by Naomi Shihab Nye (Aladdin Paperbacks).

As you share the beauty of these rhymes with your class, consult an atlas or globe to find the country represented by each poem, providing context and perspective for the children. Invite your students to place a colored push pin in the map to show the location of each rhyme. And, above all, enjoy the wealth of words this world has to offer you and your children.

"The greatest discovery of my generation is that human beings can alter their lives by altering their attitude."
—William James

Il Etait Une Dame Tartine

(*There Was a Dame Called Tartine/* A French Nursery Rhyme)

There was an old dame called Tartine
Who had a house made of butter and cream.
Its walls were of flour, it is said,
And its floors were of gingerbread!

Her bed she did make
Of white frosted cake;
And her pillow at night
Was a biscuit so light!

☆ Activities ☆

* What a delicious image this French nursery rhyme creates! It is the perfect opportunity to inspire children to create their own magical houses. Ask: What would your house be made of? Give children art materials so they can draw or construct their homes. Suggest that students write or dictate a rhyme or story about their houses.

* If your class has a sweet tooth, try making a house of treats like the one described in the nursery rhyme. Children can collaborate on creating a large model of Dame Tartine's house. A variety of purchased cookies can be "glued" together with canned frosting. Don't forget the gingerbread!

Er Waren Drie Eendjes in een Pontje

(*Three Duckies in a Brook*/ A Dutch Nursery Rhyme)

There were three duckies in a brookie
One called Bookie,
One called Gookie
And one called Klip-Klap-Keppelookie.

Klip-Klap-Keppelookie found a cookie
But he would not give it to Bookie.
So Bookie took a stone and peg
And hit Klip-Klap-Keppelookie in the leg!

"For shame, Bookie,"
Then said Gookie,
"To take a stone and peg
And hit Klip-Klap-Keppelookie in the leg!"

☆Activities☆

✳ This is an "odd duck" of a rhyme! It's almost more of a story than a rhyme, yet it does have the qualities of traditional nursery rhymes: silly characters with funny names and a strong moral. Invite children to compare this rhyme with the nursery rhymes they are more familiar with.

✳ Invite children to extend the rhyme by adding characters that rhyme with "Bookie." What if there were five little ducks? What would their names be? What else might happen?

✳ Use the rhyme as a springboard to discuss appropriate and inappropriate behaviors. Ask: What could Bookie do instead of hitting? What could Klip-Klap-Keppelookie do differently?

Russian Nursery Rhyme

Little bells, pretty flowers of the steppes
Turning your faces my way.
Why do you droop your heads
On such a bright May day?

As you shake your heads in the grasses
What do you whisper and say?

Snail, snail
Shakety shake
Put out your horns
And I'll give you some cake!

☆Activities☆

* This rhyme suggests images of Russia in spring as the new flowers bravely peak up through the cold, flat steppes. Check the school library, the Internet, and *National Geographic* magazines to find photos of Russia that can help to fix these images in the children's minds. What else do you notice in the pictures? How can these images be added to the rhyme?

* Do flowers actually talk to snails? Invite children to consider this question, and have them imagine the flowers talking to other animals and insects. What might the flowers say to each living thing? Rewrite the last stanza to reflect students' ideas.

Klokken Fem Melker Mari

(*Mary Milks the Cow*/A Norse Rhyme)

Tick tock, five o'clock, Mary milks the cow.
Mary milks as fast as she can, as fast as she can, can, can.

Tick tock, six o'clock, Mary pours the milk.
Mary pours the milk in the pan, the milk in the pan, pan, pan.

Tick tock, seven o'clock, the milk is in the cart
And horsey draws the cart along, cloperty, cloperty, clop.

Tick tock, eight o'clock, baby drinks his milk.
Baby drinks it every drop, drinks it every drop.

☆Activities☆

∗ In this Norse rhyme, one can almost hear the rhythmic ticking of the clock. Give a small group of children rhythm sticks and claves to tick off the beat as other children say the rhyme while walking around the room. At the end of each stanza children can stop and pantomime the actions suggested in the rhyme.

∗ After listening to the rhyme, children may be interested in learning more about milking cows. How do people milk cows? How does the milk get to children's cereal bowls for breakfast? Do some library research together to find out. Children will learn that there are still some farmers in the United States who "hand milk" their cows as Mary does, but there are other methods too.

∗ Show students what five o'clock, six o'clock, seven o'clock, and eight o'clock look like—both on a traditional clock with hands and a digital clock.

Round Is My Bun

(A Hungarian Nursery Rhyme)

Round is my bun—yum, yum.
My pocket's too small for my bun—yum, yum.

Break it in two, will that do?
It fits, it fits! Hurrah for you!

☆Activities☆

* This is a good example of a problem-solving rhyme. The character faces a problem and must find a way to solve it. Discuss other ways to solve the problem. If you had a delicious bun that was too big for your pocket, what would you do? (Most kids will eat it!) What if you had a rock that was too big? Hmmmmmm....

* Use a toaster oven to make simple buns for snack time. If you don't have time or energy to make them from scratch, then use store-bought refrigerator sweet buns dough. Suggest that children say the rhyme and act it out as they are eating their snacks!

The Drums Call the Village to Dance

(A South African Rhyme)

The drums call the village to dance.
I'm coming today to dance.
Tum, tum, tum, tum, goes the drum!

☆Activities☆

* Can you hear the drum beat in this rhyme? It shines through the few but expressive words. Get out the class drums to accompany the reciting of the rhyme. Children can experiment with beating the drum on each word for a steady beat. After children learn how to keep the beat, invite them to create another rhythm to go with the words. For example, words with two syllables (village, coming, today) can get two fast beats.

* Create simple drums out of coffee cans, salt or oatmeal cylinder boxes, or plastic containers. Encourage the children to decorate their drums in a way that represents their personalities and interests. Children may put photo collages on the side of the drums and paste on stickers, fabric scraps, items from nature, and art materials. Have children write their names on their drums and take them home at the end of the year.

* Is there a family member or teacher in your school who plays the drum? Invite him or her to play for your class and give simple lessons. Don't forget to dance, dance, dance!

Sleep My Baby, Sleep an Hour

(A Romanian Lullaby)

Sleep my baby, sleep an hour.
You're my little gillyflower.
Mother rocks you, mother's near.
She will wash you, baby dear
Wash you clean in water clear
Keep the sunshine from you, hear?
Sleep my baby, sleep an hour.
Grow up like a gillyflower!

☆Activities☆

* What is it about a lullaby that sounds so comforting? Invite children to share the feelings that arise from listening to this rhyme. Ask: How does it make you feel? Why?

* Use this lovely Romanian lullaby as an introduction to other lullabies. Invite children to share the lullabies they remember from infancy. Invite family members to visit and share their traditional lullabies with the group. Write these on chart paper, illustrate them, and publish a class "Lullabies Around the World" big book.

* Bring out the baby dolls and create a baby nursery in the dramatic play area. Children can memorize this lullaby and other ones to sing and rock the dolls to sleep.

Away, Way Off

(A West African Rhyme)

Child, I must sweep the hut today.
Sisters, grind the meal I pray.
To hunt the elephants Father's gone.
On the elephant hunt the Chief has gone.
Little Cuma climbs a tree
Watching the road he sings, sings he,
"It's far where my father's gone today
Away, way off, away and away!"

☆Activities☆

* This is a "story" rhyme that paints a vivid picture of life many years ago in West Africa. Talk with the children about the picture they hear in the story. What was life like in West Africa at the time this rhyme was made? Collect and display present-day photos of West African cities and villages for children to observe and compare. It is important for children to know that, today, African countries have some very modern living areas— much like the United States.

* Invite children to pantomime the actions of the rhyme as it is being said. Suggest that children create and collect props from the dramatic play and art areas to illustrate the roles. Ask: What are the chores your family does around the home? Can we rewrite the rhyme using these chores?

ABC die Katz'lief in den Schnee

(A German Nursery Rhyme)

ABC, Kitty's in the snow, I see!
When she comes back home again
She has little white boots then!
O Jimminy! O Jo!

ABC, Kitty climbs a tree.
She licks her little cold, cold feet.
She cleans her booties off so neat
And goes no more out in the snow!
O Jimminy! O Jo!

☆Activities☆

* This is a great opportunity to invite children to talk about their winter experiences! Ask: Have you ever experienced snow? Do you like to go out and play in the snow? Do cats like the snow (not usually!)? What about other animals?

* Look at the title of the rhyme. Ask the children to guess which German word is kitty and which is snow. Ask: What clues did you use to help you guess?

* Encourage children to extend the rhyme by using some of the people and animals they talked about above. For example:

    ABC, Doggie's in the snow, I see!
    When he comes back home again
    He'll have a very wet tail then!
    O Jimminy! O Jo!

Die Liese Kommt Gelaufen

(Little Liese Comes A-Running/A German Nursery Rhyme)

Little Liese comes a-running.
Who'll buy my little calf?
How much do you want for him?
A penny and a half!

A penny and a half's too much.
A broomstick's all I'll pay.
Then take him for a broomstick;
I don't want him anyway!

☆Activities☆

* Ask children to look at the title to find a word that matches a word in the rhyme. Explain that "Liese" is a child's name. Invite children to sound out the other German words in the title and match them to words in the English translation. For example, does "kommt" sound a bit like "come"? Children will be thrilled to know these few words in German!

* What else does little Liese have to sell? Children can create their own rhymes by adding new verses about other animals and things for sale. The trick for children is to create a rhyme for the sale item at the end of the fourth line. For example:

> Little Liese comes a-running.
> Who'll buy my lovely beehive?
> How much do you want for it?
> A dollar twenty five!
>
> A dollar twenty five is too much.
> A banana is all I'll pay!
> Then take it for a banana.
> I don't want it anyway!

Le Bon Roi Dagobert

(A French Nursery Rhyme)

King Dagobert once wore
His breeches turned hindside before.
Said Eloi, the friar:
"Oh my King and Sire,
Those breeches on you
Are all wrongside to!"
The King said, "You don't say!
Then I'll turn the other way!"

☆Activities☆

* The absurdity of this rhyme makes it fun for children, but most children will need your help to actually get the joke. You might want to illustrate the joke in a fun way by putting on a jacket backwards when you introduce the rhyme. Of course, when reading the last line, turn around for the full effect!

* Use this rhyme to launch a "Backwards Day" at your school. Invite children to suggest things the class could do and say backwards on the special day. Ideas might include: Greet each other by saying "good-bye;" walk backwards around the room; take attendance in reverse alphabetical order.

Sleep, Sleep, My Little One

(An Abysinnian/East African Lullaby)

Sleep, sleep, my little one,
The night is all wind and rain.
The meal has been wet by the raindrops,
And bent is the sugar cane.
O Giver who gives to the people,
In safety my little son keep.
My little son with headdress, sleep, sleep, sleep!

☆Activities☆

* Here is another lullaby to share with the children. Can you hear the raindrops? Put out a pan of water, eyedroppers, and a few sprinkling cans. Invite children to create rain sound effects to accompany the speaking of the lullaby.

* Have children compare this lullaby to the Romanian lullaby on page 100. How are the two rhymes the same? (Both use water.) How are they different? (In the Romanian rhyme, a mother is washing her baby; in this one, the water comes from rain.)

Hi Yi Hy Yi Hytola

(A Finnish Rhyme)

Hi Yi Hy Yi Hytola
The dogs of Hytola bark.
My little girls, my little boys
Hear them coming! Hark!

✫Activities✫

✳ Ask children to clap the rhythm of the rhyme as they say it, as if they are clapping to call the dogs home.

✳ Use a large atlas or globe to find the country of Finland. Collect pictures of Finland so children can compare this country's appearance with their own area. How is it the same or different? (You will find many beautiful pictures on the Internet and in children's nonfiction books; you might also ask a travel agent if he or she can spare a free travel brochure on Finland.)

Row, Row to the Fishing Banks Fair

(A Norse Rhyme)

Row, row to the fishing banks fair!
How many fishes did you catch there?
One for father, one for mother,
One for sister, one for brother,
And one for the little fisher boy!

☆Activities☆

* If you have a small class and happen to live close to a fishing spot, a natural extension to this Norse rhyme is to take youngsters fishing. Even children as young as 4 or 5 years old can appreciate the thrill of casting a line and waiting for a bite. Often, local Trout Unlimited chapters or sport fishing companies will donate used rods and lures. Check with your local 4-H club as well; they may be able to supply you with one or two trained volunteers. Invite parents or other relatives along too; the more adults you have to help, the better. Be prepared for some tangled lines—and be sure to bring an extra dose of patience! Even if you don't catch a thing, it will be an exciting experience.

* If you can't take children fishing, try to get hold of a film strip or photos of people fishing. You can also bring the experience into the dramatic play area. One option is to bring a small canoe or dingy into the classroom for a few days. Add life preservers, homemade reels, vests, and other fishing gear, and let children act out a fishing trip. To make the experience complete, children can make paper fish to "catch."

* Ask: How many fish would *you* need to catch to feed everyone in your house? (A great counting lesson!)

* Provide books and magazines on fishing for children to browse through.

The Earth Is Your Mother

(A Native American Lullaby)

The earth is your mother she holds you
The sky is your father he protects you
The winds are your brothers they sing to you
Rainbow is your sister she loves you
Sleep, sleep, we are together always
Sleep, sleep, there never was a time
When this was not so.

☆ Activities ☆

✳ This is a perfect chant to recite right before rest time, or at other
moments when children need to calm down. To help children think
about the earth and the elements around them, ask them to think
about their favorite places on the earth (maybe their houses or yards, a
local park or a special tree). Record students responses on a language
experience chart: "Maggie's favorite place on earth is...her mother's
garden./Jonah's favorite place on earth is...his hideout under the
stairs./Elena's favorite place on earth is...in her mother's lap."

✳ Extend the activity by asking children to observe the world around
them a bit more closely. For example, ask: What color is the sky in the
morning? What color is it in the afternoon? What color is it after dinner? What color is it at bedtime? What color is it when there is a rainbow? Invite students to paint their observations.

Japanese Lullaby

Sleep my baby, Sleep my baby.
Where is nursie gone?
Away, way over the mountaintops,
Nursie has gone home.
And from her little village
What will nursie bring?

A drum, rub-a-dub, and a flute of bamboo.
A tumble-down dolly that stands straight for you
And a small paper dog on a string!

✫Activities✫

* Have props ready before you introduce this rhyme. Place the drum, doll, flute, and paper dog on a string inside a "mystery box" at circle time or small group time. Sing the rhyme together, and when you get to the line, "What will nursie bring?" pull out the props one at a time.

* To extend the activity, ask one child at a time to play "nursie" and find something new to put in the box. Encourage them not to let anyone else see it! After the new item has been added, sing the rhyme again and pull out what the child brought. Be sure to end the rhyme with "a small paper dog on a string," however, for the sake of continuity.

Happy the Dark Winter Day

(An Inuit Rhyme)

I-yay! I-yuy! I-yay!
Happy the dark winter day!
Then come friends from afar.
Happy how happy we are.
Tat-a-tat-tat! Drums beat like that.
Friends and our villagers dance away!
Yay-yay, we sing, yay, yay, yay, yay.
Happy, how happy, the dark winter day!

☆Activities☆

✳ This rhyme is filled with exuberance for a dark winter day—the same type of day which many of us would complain about! Use this rhyme on a dark, dreary day in January or February to liven up the classroom. Share a winter picnic (indoors or out). Get out your drums and sing and dance this joyful rhyme.

✳ Explain that the Inuit people live in the Arctic, the icy region at the top of the globe. There are times during the Arctic winter that the sun does not shine all day long! Ask students to imagine what that lifestyle might be like.

THERE WAS AN OLD WOMAN

(A Chinese Rhyme)

There was an old woman,
As I have heard tell,
She went to sell pie,
But her pie would not sell.

She hurried back home,
But her door-step was high,
She stumbled and fell
And a dog ate her pie!

☆Activities☆

✳ Chanting a rhyme like this one over and over invites children to enter the realm of rhythm. It doesn't matter so much what the words say as how the cadence of the verse rolls off the tongue. Invite children to change some of the words after they have become familiar with the rhyme. For instance: "There was an old woman as I have heard tell, she went to sell eggs but her eggs would not sell, She hurried back home but her door step was high, She stumbled and fell and her eggs all got FRIED!" Encourage children to be silly!

THERE WAS A LITTLE BOY

(A Chinese Rhyme)

There was a little boy
Who climbed a pile of dirt;
He found a piece of money
But fell and wasn't hurt;
He bought rice and salt
That would make you laugh
Enough to last his mother
A whole year and a half.

☆ Activities ☆

✳ As you sing this rhyme at circle time or small group time, pass around a cup of uncooked rice for children to touch.

✳ Set up a treasure hunt inside your classroom or outdoors. Hide (real or toy) coins inside the sand table and all about the room, or outside in the grass. Invite children to hunt for the money. Set up a "Chinese market" in the dramatic play area with baskets and bags of rice, chopsticks, and other appropriate props. After children have found the hidden money, invite them to go to "market" to purchase bags of rice or other goods with their coins. Provide a variety of sizes of rice bags from which children can choose. You may even want to trace 2 or 3 coin sizes on bags so children can match the number of coins to the right bag for purchasing.

✳ Extend the activity by cooking rice with the children and eating it for lunch or snack. Make chopsticks available at your mealtimes so children can choose to use them if they like.

THE MOUSE AND THE CANDLESTICK

(A Chinese Rhyme/Sung Up the Scale)

(Do) The mouse climbed up the candlestick

(Re) To steal the tallow from the wick.

(Mi) When he got up he couldn't get down;

(Fa) He called so loud he waked the town.

(So) He called for the cat but the cat wouldn't come,

(La) So he called for his mother to take him home.

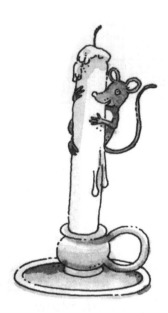

☆Activities☆

✳ Sing this rhyme beginning at the bottom of the scale in a soft voice. Get louder as you go and, when you get to the last line, shout it! After the children have learned the rhyme well and shouted as loud as they can, try reciting it backwards. Start loud and end very, very softly back at the first line.

✳ Place a lighted or unlighted candle (depending on school rules, class size, and safety concerns) in the center of your circle as a prop.

GIUSEPPE THE COBBLER

(An Italian Rhyme)

Giuseppi the cobbler makes my shoes;
He pounds them, rap, rap, rap!
He makes them small, he makes them big,
And ever he pounds, tap, tap.

☆Activities☆

* After you teach this simple little rhyme, ask children if they know what a cobbler is. Invite them to think about the people who made shoes a long time ago and how they did it. Show pictures of cobblers in storybooks and if you can, bring in some old-fashioned shoes to show children. Then invite children to take off one of their own shoes and look at it carefully. Ask: Who do you think made your shoe? What holds your shoe together? Pass the shoes around at circle or small group time and discuss how they are the same and different.

* Extend the lesson by placing chart paper on the floor and creating a large shoe graph. See how many different ways students can "chart" their shoes: by color, size, shape, buckles versus laces, leather versus rubber, etc.

MARIO, MARIETTA, AND VANNO

(An Italian Rhyme)

Mario, Marietta, and Vanno
Went to the fair today;
They each brought back a pumpkin,
But I stayed home to play.

✧ Activities ✧

✳ This little verse is a perfect one for autumn and is fun to sing on the way to the pumpkin farm. However, it can be also be used for planning time in the classroom. First, make sure students become familiar with the verse and are singing it a lot throughout the day. Then, the next day, instead of asking children what they are going to play that day, sing or chant this little verse and ask three children at a time to go to the area where they'd like to BEGIN their play and bring back something from that area. One might go to the dramatic play area and bring back a hat, another to the block corner for a block or to the easel for a paintbrush. Each time, incorporate the children's names and the items they choose into the song. For instance, your rhyme might sound something like this:

> *Jamal, Alesa, and Colin*
> *Went to the fair today!*
> *They brought back a....*
> *BLOCK, A PAINTBRUSH, AND A HAT*
> *But I stayed home to play!*

LUCY LOCKET

(A Traditional British Rhyme)

Lucy Locket, lost her pocket
Kitty Fisher found it;
There was not a penny in it,
But a ribbon round it.

☆Activities☆

* You can chant this simple verse slowly and ask the children to go on a hunt for a "pocket" (coin purse, small box, cloth pouch) around the room or outside. Put a variety of coins and different numbers of coins in each "pocket" for children to discover. Then tell children all to close their eyes again and hunt for another "pocket" with different coins inside! Ask them if they can count the items inside their "pockets." You can vary the items inside, too...they don't have to be coins. They could be ribbons, feathers, stones or a whole variety of interesting objects that children can use in later play. It's fun if they relate to a theme you are using in the classroom that day.

* This can be a fun activity to do with children in pairs as well. Ask children to pair up; have one be Lucy Locket and the other Kitty Fisher. Hide the "pockets" again and let children look for them together. When they've found their "pockets," ask them to join their partner, put all their coins together, and count them! This is a good way to promote cooperation and leadership. The children who can count well will help the ones who are still learning.

Snack Time Rhymes

Have you ever noticed that rhymes and songs can create order out of chaos? Start singing a rhyme as children are launching into their cacophonous chorus of snack time demands, and you will find that what once was "noise" has become a unison of "song" with purpose. You may even want to keep a few favorite snack rhymes on laminated cards in your pocket for quick reference when the children are getting a bit too silly. What a great way to avert an impending food fight! And you need not stop with the rhymes in this section. Many of the songs and rhymes you use for circle time can be adapted for snack time. In many ways, snack time is like circle time with food!

Whether you are singing to get the children's attention, to give a direction, or just for fun, the power of rhyme and music will infuse your "delicious" gathering with a sense of order and harmony.

**"The first of all considerations is that our meals
shall be fun as well as fuel."
—Andre Simon**

THIS LITTLE HAND

(A Washing-Up Rhyme)

This little hand is my right hand.
(Hold up right hand.)
This little hand is its brother.
(Hold up left hand.)
Together, they wash, and they wash, and they wash,
(Pretend to wash hands.)
One hand washes the other!

☆Activities☆

* Hand washing is probably part of your core curriculum; it is certainly something that happens many times each day. Use this rhyme to turn hand-washing into a game instead of drudgery.

* If your children have not yet learned to distinguish right from left, don't worry about it. Let them hold up whichever hand they want while singing the rhyme. Once children have had time to enjoy the rhyme, use it to teach the important concept of right and left.

* Ask: Why is it important to wash hands? Most young children think it is just something that adults tell you to do! Talk to your class about germs and sickness. There are many simple books about hand washing and germs available. Read one to your class!

PUT THE TOYS AWAY

(Tune: *Mary Had Little Lamb*)

  (child's name) , put the toys away,
Toys away,
Toys away.
  (child's name) , put the toys away,
Time for snack!

☆Activities☆

You've probably had this or a similar experience: You glance at the clock while your students are playing and realize it's already ten minutes past your regular snack time. You need to get the room straightened and the food served quickly—before hunger and crankiness set in. Use this rhyme in just such moments to engage the whole class in cleaning up. Children can't resist hearing their own names sung, and they will do anything you ask them to!

CLEAN-UP TIME

(Tune: *Good Night Ladies*)

Clean up, __(first child's name)__ ,
Clean up, __(second child's name)__ ,
Clean up, __(third child's name)__ ,
It's time for our snack!

⭐Activities⭐

Turn clean-up into a game!   First, sing this song as a signal that clean-up time has arrived. Have children in each area of the room work together to straighten up. As soon as they think their areas are clean, they should sit on the floor. This is a signal that they are ready for inspection. Have them straighten or put away anything they missed, then do another inspection. When their area is clean and neat, the team may be excused to snack or the next activity. This is an excellent way for children to gain a sense of group responsibility.

SNACK TIME RHYME

Bend them, stretch them.
(Close and open hands two times.)
Give a little clap.
(Clap hands.)
Bend them, stretch them.
(Close and open hands two times.)
Put them in your lap!

First I sit in my chair,
Now I put my hands in the air.
I lower them slowly to my lap,
Now I'm ready for my snack.

☆Activities☆

This is an enjoyable way to make sure children are seated and keeping their hands to themselves so that you can start serving the day's snack. Have the children follow the instructions in the song. Look carefully to see who is sitting quietly with hands in lap; consider serving these students first. Soon, everyone will rush to follow the instructions in the rhyme.

POLLY, PUT THE KETTLE ON

Polly, put the kettle on,
Polly, put the kettle on,
Polly, put the kettle on,
We'll all have tea.

Sukey, take it off again,
Sukey, take it off again,
Sukey, take it off again,
They've all gone away.

☆Activities☆

* Sing this one with the children who are playing in the dramatic play area. Encourage them to think about how one treats visitors. Act like a visitor, let them serve you a snack, and be sure to thank them for their hospitality!

* There are plenty of danger areas in the kitchen, including kettles and pots of boiling water. If you prepare a snack or lunch that involves piping-hot liquid or food, be sure to talk about safety.

* Encourage the children to think about the sequence of steps you must follow when you are preparing a snack. For example, to make hot water for tea, you must fill the kettle, put it on the stove, wait for it to boil, then take it off again. Ask children to think about what would happen if you skipped a step or did it out of sequence.

BLOW, WIND, BLOW

Blow, wind, blow!
Go, mill, go!
The miller must grind his corn
So the baker may take it
And into bread bake it,
And bring us a loaf in the morn.

☆Activities☆

* Talk about where bread comes from. Many children think it comes from the supermarket, and will need the terms "baker" and "miller" explained to them.

* Find pictures of different kinds of bread to show the children and discuss the breads the students have tried at home. Better still, bring in some samples of different breads for the children to try.

* Make bread with the children. If you don't have time to make it from scratch, use a frozen bread dough. Children can at least see how the bread rises and bakes!

WHO STOLE THE COOKIES?

Who stole the cookies from the cookie jar?
Who, me? Yes, you!
Couldn't be! Then who?

 (child's name)   stole the cookies from the cookie jar.
Who, me? Yes, you!
Couldn't be! Then who?

(Repeat with other student's names.)

☆Activities☆

This well-loved chant is a great way to help students remember one another's names. Use a drum to keep the beat or ask children to clap a steady beat on their knees. When you sing a child's name, invite him or her to choose another child's name for the next round.

PAT-A-CAKE

Pat-a-cake, pat-a-cake, baker's man,
Bake me a cake as fast as you can;
Roll it and prick it and mark it with B,
And put it in the oven for baby and me!

☆Activities☆

* Many of your students will remember this beloved nursery rhyme from babyhood. Review the hand motions that accompany the rhyme and let children play pat-a-cake with each other.

* Sing this rhyme together when you bake a cake or pie in the classroom. Use raisins or frosting to mark your cake with a "B."

* Turn this rhyme into an alphabet rhyme! Instead of singing "B" and "baby," sing each child's first name along with its initial letter. (It does not matter that many letters will not rhyme with the word "me.") This is an excellent way to review initial consonant and vowel sounds.

IF I HAD AN APPLE

(Tune: *If I Had a Hammer*)

If I had an apple,
I'd eat it in the morning,
I'd eat it in the evening,
All over this land.
I'd eat it for breakfast,
I'd eat it for supper,
I'd eat with all my friends, my sister, and my brothers
All, all over this land.

☆Activities☆

* Go on a class field trip to an orchard, and pick some apples straight from the trees. Most orchards label the different varieties of apples growing in the rows, and you can have great fun comparing the way the apples look and taste. If a field trip is out of the question, bring in several apple varieties from the grocery store or farmer's market and do the same comparison activity.

* Invite children to change the rhyme to incorporate their own favorite foods. For example, a child might sing, "If I had a watermelon," or "If I had a french fry."

HOT CROSS BUNS

Hot cross buns,
Hot cross buns.
One a penny,
Two a penny,
Hot cross buns!

If you have no penny,
A farthing will do;
If you have no farthing
Then God bless you.

☆Activities☆

* In Britain, hot cross buns are sold at Easter time . These treats are spicy rolls made from yeast dough, sometimes with raisins or a sugar glaze on top. A dough cross is baked on the top of each bun. Use frozen bread or bun dough to make some buns for students to sample. Children love to make things from dough and bread dough can take all the handling!

* Create a class bakery in the dramatic play area. Make playdough buns and sell them for pennies! Create prices and advertisement signs to illustrate the store.

JIMMY CRACK CORN

Jimmy crack corn, but I don't care.
Jimmy crack corn, but I don't care.
Jimmy crack corn, but I don't care.
My master's gone away.

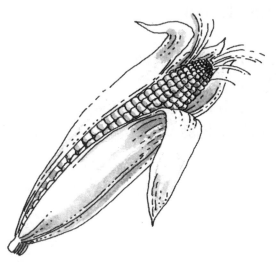

☆Activities☆

* Bring in an ear of corn (preferably still in its husk) to show students how this crop grows. Ask: What could Jimmy be doing as he "cracks" the corn? Is he cutting ears off the corn plant? Taking kernels of corn off the cob? Have students use their imaginations.

* Bring in a few varieties of dried corn and provide children with tools to "crack" the corn or take it off the cob. Provide magnifying glasses so that students can look closely at the kernels.

* After children crack the corn, provide them with glue and paper to make a corn collage. The more colors, the better!

* Make corn pudding or corn bread with the children.

* Take the children on a field trip to a cornfield and a granary to see how the corn is grown and stored.

PEASE PORRIDGE HOT

Pease porridge hot,
Pease porridge cold,
Pease porridge in the pot,
Nine days old.

Some like it hot,
Some like it cold,
Some like it in the pot,
Nine days old.

☆Activities☆

* What is porridge? Explain that porridge is a type of hot cereal, somewhat like oatmeal. Talk about oatmeal. What do the children like to serve on their oatmeal? Milk, maple syrup, fruit, applesauce, cinnamon? Make a list of the children's ideas and use them for snack the next day. Make instant oatmeal and set out the toppings "salad bar style" for children to mix/match and serve themselves. While eating you can ask: "Would you want to eat anything that is nine days old?"

* Create rhyme inventions with the second verse. How else do people like their porridge? The lines do not have to rhyme, just be silly and fun! "Some like it sweet, Some like it sour, Some like it in the pot, nine days old" -OR- "Some like it lumpy, some like it bumpy, Some like it in the pot, nine days jumpy!"

LITTLE TOMMY TUCKER

Little Tommy Tucker
Sings for his supper.
What shall we give him?
White bread and butter.
How shall he cut it
Without e're a knife?
How shall he marry
Without e're a wife?

☆Activities☆

This rhyme can serve as a simple introduction to things that "go together." After children become familiar with this little chant, play an association game with them: Set out several items on a tray that obviously go together, such as bread and butter, a key and a padlock, a nail and a hammer, a teacup and a teapot, a baby doll and a baby bottle. Mix the items up and have children take turns matching them up. You can easily turn this into a math activity by asking children to count the items separately. Then after they are "paired up" ask them to count the pairs!

Alphabet Rhymes

Young children enjoy repeating funny sounds and putting words together in silly combinations. They often try to rhyme each other's names as in "Ellen, Ellen Watermelon," or play with the initial sounds of names as in "Mighty Magic Max." The following literacy poems are designed to take advantage of this special interest of preschoolers and use it to introduce phonemic awareness. What better way for children to learn about the sounds that letters make than by "playing" with words just as children do naturally?

One of the ways children play with words is to repeat words and phrases over and over again. They seem to know instinctively that repetition is one of the best methods of learning! These alliterative poems utilize children's love of repetition in a constructive (and sometimes absurd!) learning situation.

Before you introduce a new poem to the children, it is best to get to know it yourself. Practice saying it until the rhythm and emotion is clear. Think about ways you can set the mood or scene for the poem. Visual aids such as felt-board pieces, posters, or props can be used to set the stage. Discussing the scene that is portrayed in the poem will help prepare children to listen.

Once the mood is set, read the entire poem to the children. Of course, the more dramatic and rhythmic your reading, the better! When children have heard the poem once, they will be eager to join you in chanting it. These poems are call-and-response poems; you recite the verse (or first line), and students recite the chorus (or response line). Be prepared for plenty of giggles and smiles—many of the chorus lines are humorous tongue twisters! Once children are familiar with the poem, discuss it. Are there words children do not know? Discussing unfamiliar words can help clarify the meaning of the poem and expand children's vocabulary.

Even though most preschoolers and kindergartners can't read, many are interested in letters. Make rhyme charts for each of the poems so children can see the words that have the alliterative letters. They will soon find more words with the letters throughout the school!

"The noblest pleasure is the joy of understanding."
—Leonardo da Vinci

ABSURD ACTING ACROBATS

by Ellen Booth Church

Who's that flying on the trapeze?
    Absurd acting acrobats!

Laughing and spinning around with ease.
    Absurd acting acrobats!

By the look of their costumes and their strange sounds.
    Absurd acting acrobats!

They're not really acrobats, they must be clowns!
    Absurd acting acrobats!

☆Activities☆

* Have a class circus! Create it in the dramatic play area with costumes and props. Then recite the poem over and over again!

* Ask students if anyone has ever seen a circus. Do they know what an acrobat does? Allow time for students to share their experiences.

* Just for fun, have students brainstorm a list of possible circus animals that start with the letter "A." Ants, anteaters, alligators, angora cats, aardvarks, and amphibians are a few possibilities. Check a children's dictionary or other books for more.

ANGRY ACTING ANTS

by Ellen Booth Church

What's going on at the anthill today?
　　Angry acting ants.

Running around with no time to play.
　　Angry acting ants.

Do you see what could make them so upset?
　　Angry acting ants.

It's a big anteater who's making a threat.
　　Angry acting ants.

☆Activities☆

* Have the children ever really watched ants in action? Take a few different types of crumbs and honey outside to attract ants to a side area of the playground. Put out the food. A few minutes later, watch the circus-like antics begin!

* Ask: What is an anteater? Have the children ever heard of one? What does this animal's name suggest about its favorite food? If children have never seen a picture of an anteater, invite them to draw what they think an anteater might look like. Later, show them a real picture of one from a book or the Internet.

* Turn a traditional game of tag into a game of ANTS and ANTEATER on the playground. The child who is "it" is the anteater and must tag at least one ant for dinner!

BIG BOUNCING BUBBLES

by Ellen Booth Church

What made the dog bark?
    Big bouncing bubbles!

What made the bees buzz?
    Big bouncing bubbles!

It's that bully, he's the worst!
    Big bouncing bubbles!

He made all my bubbles burst!
    Big bouncing bubbles.

☆Activities☆

* All children know what happens when someone gets too close to their beautiful bubbles...POP! Invite children to think about what this poem is about. What is a bully? What does a bully do?

* Make bubbles! Here is a simple way to make bubble pipes out of Styrofoam cups and plastic drinking straws (cut in half). Show children how to poke a hole about one third of the way up from the bottom of the cup and then insert the straw into the hole. Make a bubble mixture out of liquid dish soap, water, and glycerin (or use store-bought bubbles). Have the children set the top of the cup down in the mixture so that a film of soap forms over the mouth of the cup; when the children blow gently into the "pipe," bubbles will form!

CRAZY CRYING CATS

by Ellen Booth Church

What's that noise out at the creek?
    Crazy crying cats.

If you listen closely you can hear them speak.
    Crazy crying cats.

Now do your best to stay out of their way.
    Crazy crying cats.

When they come, they'll be running astray!
    Crazy crying cats.

☆Activities☆

✱ All of the alliterative poems in this collection have phonemic awareness words in the rhyme that match the sound of the words in the chorus. Ask: Can you find all the words that start with "c" in this poem? (Hint: creek, closely, come, crazy, crying, cats) What other words can children add that start with the "c" sound?

✱ Ask children to think about what "crazy crying cats" might say? Invite children to make up nonsense words and chants for the cats to say (using the "c" sound, preferably). Then dramatize the poem: Have a group of children chosen to be cats crying and running around the playground or gym, while other children try to stay out of their way!

DOZENS OF DANCING DONKEYS

by Ellen Booth Church

Who's that knocking at the door?
 Dozens of dancing donkeys!

One white, one gray, and many more....
 Dozens of dancing donkeys!

What's this? They're digging up the floor!
 Dozens of dancing donkeys!

Let them in, their hooves are sore!
 Dozens of dancing donkeys!

☆Activities☆

✻ Children can make pairs of donkey ears out of construction paper or oak tag. Glue on gray, white, and brown felt to give the ears a soft, furry texture. Attach them to strips of paper so children can wear them as headbands. Preschoolers love hats, headbands, and "ears," so this will be a big hit!

✻ Ask: What type of music do donkeys dance to? Country-western square dance music? Use your collective imaginations to settle on a genre of music, and play the music for your class. Let the donkey dance begin!

ELEVEN EAGER EAGLES

by Ellen Booth Church

Flying east of the mountains and over the trees,
Eleven eager eagles.

Swooping and diving and riding the breeze,
Eleven eager eagles.

Each glides through the air with exquisite grace.
Eleven eager eagles.

And then they are gone without a trace.
Eleven eager eagles.

☆Activities☆

✳ Ask: Can you feel the eagles soaring in this rhyme? Have you ever seen one? What would it feel like to fly like an eagle? Invite children to imagine soaring, swooping, and diving in the breeze. Pass out sheer scarves to use as wings, and say the rhyme again with a few children at a time "flying" around!

✳ Collect feathers and feather dusters to paint with! Put on soaring music (Mozart and Debussy are great choices) and invite children to create paintings with their gossamer wings!

ELEGANT ECHOING ELK

by Ellen Booth Church

What's that rumbling sound I hear?
Elegant echoing elk.

By the sound of their footsteps, they're bigger than deer.
Elegant echoing elk.

Here they come with their heads held high.
Elegant echoing elk.

They might run on earth but they are heard in the sky.
Elegant echoing elk.

☆Activities☆

* After you share this rhyme with children, ask if anyone has ever heard an echo. Spark students' imaginations with open-ended questions: Where do echoes come from? What makes an echo? Where do echoes live? Do they stay in one place or travel around? Are echoes lonely or happy?

* Divide your class in half and ask one half to be the callers and the other half to be the echo makers. Invite the callers to decide on one word to say at the same time together. After they call out their word, the echo makers should say it back. This activity is even more fun if the two groups can't see each other.

* If you know of a nearby gorge, cave, or overpass where you can make echoes, you may want to take a field trip there with your class. Make sure you have plenty of adult volunteers. When you get there, start calling out and listening for your echo. When you "find" the echo, give each child a chance to call to it and see what the echo says back! Ask: Whose voice is that? Why does it always say the same thing you do?

FUNNY FAT FISH

by Ellen Booth Church

You'll never believe what I saw today!
　Funny fat fish!

Fooling around, right in the way!
　Funny fat fish!

Four of them foolishly fanning a fire!
　Funny fat fish!

If you don't believe that, I guess I'm a liar!
　Funny fat fish!

✮Activities✮

✳ Ask: What's silly about this rhyme? Invite children to discuss what doesn't make sense. Do fish fool around? Where would the fire be, and how would a fish fan it?

✳ Put out materials for children to make their own "funny fat fish" out of a stuffed paper lunch bag. You will need lunch bags, rubber bands, newspapers, scissors, glue, markers, and construction paper. Children can stuff the bags with newspaper wads to make the fish fat. Then use a rubber band to close each bag, leaving a bit of the bag loose to create a full, funny tail.   Decorate the stuffed fish with markers and cut-out pieces of construction paper. Have each student present his or her fish to the group and tell what makes the fish really funny!

A GAGGLE OF GLAMOROUS GEESE

by Ellen Booth Church

Who's that strutting to the garden gate?
    A gaggle of glamorous geese.

All gussied up for an important date.
    A gaggle of glamorous geese.

Wearing gobs of glitter and glorious goo.
    A gaggle of glamorous geese.

I hope they're not going on a date with you!
    A gaggle of glamorous geese.

☆Activities☆

- Ask: What would these imaginary glamorous geese look like? What do they wear when they get all gussied up? Lots of "G" stuff, of course: Gold earrings, green glasses, ghastly golf shoes, etc. Create a class drawing of the imaginary geese, the goofier the better.

- Point out to students that "gaggle" is the word for a group of geese. Other groups of animals also have specific names: a herd of hippos, a school of fish, a flock of birds, etc. Uncover other words for groups of animals and create an experience chart to illustrate them.

- Set up a glamorous beauty parlor in the dramatic play corner with lots of pretend makeup, glitter, gaudy jewelry and sunglasses.

HERD OF HUNGRY HIPPOS

by Ellen Booth Church

Look, what's in the flower box?
    A herd of hungry hippos!

They are eating up my hollyhocks!
    A herd of hungry hippos!

See them in the lettuce garden now.
    A herd of hungry hippos!

They can't be hippos, they must be cows!
    A herd of hungry hippos!

☆Activities☆

* What would a herd of hungry hippos eat? If they stick with "H" words, they might enjoy Healthy Honey Kisses. To make this treat for snack time, mix together 1 cup honey, 2 cups peanut butter, and 2 cups dry milk. Knead with clean hands and shape into the letter "H." Or shape the dough into objects that start with "H." Eat the kisses right away or chill to set the candy.

* Act out the rhyme, inviting half the children to be the herd of hungry hippos, and the others the gardeners. What does a herd of hungry hippos sound like? Encourage children to create sounds to go with their movements.

* What are hollyhocks? Take a class trip to the library to find out. (They are flowers.)

* Bring in seed catalogs and wildlife magazines for children to peruse. Have children cut out pictures to create a giant mural garden. Use markers to draw hungry hippos scattered throughout the garden.

INCREDIBLY ITCHY IGUANA

by Ellen Booth Church

What's that scratching sound I hear?
Incredibly itchy iguana.

Something is bugging him, it does appear.
Incredibly itchy iguana.

What could have happened to make him so ill?
Incredibly itchy iguana.

He fell on a cactus and rolled down the hill!
Incredibly itchy iguana.

☆Activities☆

* This is a fun call-and-response rhyme which is sure to bring out the giggles in your group. As you say the rhyme and children repeat the "incredibly itchy iguana" line, ask them to pretend they are all itchy iguanas! Ask everyone to itch furiously on this line—then stop and freeze when you say your part. As children repeat their line again, the furious itching can begin anew.

* Bring a cactus into your classroom and invite children to look at it carefully. When they've had a good look show children how sharp the prickles are on a cactus. Ask students to think about what it might feel like to fall on a cactus.

* Provide books about the desert for children to look through or take a class trip to a pet store and visit the iguanas!

JUMPING JUICY JELLYBEANS

by Ellen Booth Church

Jason jiggled open the jar!
    Jumping juicy jellybeans.

Now they're bouncing near and far!
    Jumping juicy jellybeans.

Catch them, Jim; catch them, Jill!
    Jumping juicy jellybeans.

Before that jaguar eats his fill!
    Jumping juicy jellybeans.

☆Activities☆

Make "jumping jellybean" paintings using real jellybeans or colorful marbles. You will need a few gift boxes, paper cut to fit the inside of the box, paint in bowls, marbles, and plastic spoons. First, drop the jelly-beans (or marbles) in the paint to cover. Then spoon them onto the paper in the bottom of the box. The children can then pick up the boxes and carefully tilt them back and forth, making the marbles, rock, roll, and jump! Help each child remove the jellybeans and hang the paper to dry. You will have a colorful jumping jellybean painting!

KIND KING KANGAROO

by Ellen Booth Church

Who takes the time to kiss a kitten?
   Kind King Kangaroo.

Who keeps a kite inside his kitchen?
   Kind King Kangaroo.

He loves to joke with kids all day....
   Kind King Kangaroo.

He smiles and laughs as he watches them play!
   Kind King Kangaroo.

☆Activities☆

* Ask: How many "k" words can you find in this rhyme? Count them together, then ask children to suggest other objects that start with the sound of "k" for the King to keep in his kitchen. Use them in the rhyme.

* What foods could the King cook that start with the letter "k"? Make an experience chart listing them and create a "krazy" recipe book of "k" foods.

* Make Kind King Kangaroo Kites! Use a small paper lunch bag, kite string and tape to create a handmade box style kite. Show children how to roll down the top edge of the bag about one inch to reinforce it. Then have children tape six-inch long strings to each of the four corners of the bag edge. Tie the ends together and add to a long piece of string for pulling through the air. Decorate with "k" objects and, of course, the letter itself!

LOST LITTLE LION

by Ellen Booth Church

Do you hear a low whimper from that log?
    Lost little lion!

It looks like a lump in the lake bog!
    Lost little lion!

But wait—I think it is starting to go....
    Lost little lion!

Hurry home, little lion, your mom's full of woe!
    Lost little lion!

☆Activities☆

* Invite children to tell the story of the rhyme in their own words. Where is the rhyme taking place? What is happening? How does the little lion feel? Did you ever feel like this? Talk about the feeling of getting lost and the safe things to do if that happens.

* Discuss any new words that children encounter in the poem. What is a bog? A whimper? Woe? Write them on an experience chart with synonyms.

MILLIONS OF MAGICAL MICE

by Ellen Booth Church

This morning I saw right out my window...
    Millions of magical mice.

Casting spells and making up tricks.
    Millions of magical mice.

With magnets and mirrors, they make their pranks work.
    Millions of magical mice.

Watch your step, you won't know where they lurk!
    Millions of magical mice.

☆Activities☆

* Make magic-mice finger puppets for acting out the rhyme! Children can use fingers from old gloves, peanut shells, or toilet paper tubes. Decorate each one with magician's gear, such as a top hat, magic wand, and mirrors.

* Make "magic mirror" pictures. Invite children to draw or paint half of a face or body on a piece of paper. Then stand a mirror on the central line of the picture to see it magically completed!

* Magnet art is great fun. Dip metal objects such as paper clips, washers, or ball bearings in paint and place on plain paper sitting on a thin piece of cardboard. Place a strong magnet under the cardboard and move it around in order to move the metal objects around on the paper. A beautiful painting will be your end product!

MANY MARVELOUS MONSTERS

by Ellen Booth Church

With hats and scarves and wonderful junk,
    Many marvelous monsters.
They turn into creatures and maybe a skunk!
    Many marvelous monsters.
Then with a tip of the hat and a wave of the hand,
    Many marvelous monsters.
They take off for their very own fantasy land.
    Many marvelous monsters.
Flying east of the buildings and over the trees,
    Many marvelous monsters.
They just always do whatever they please!
    Many marvelous monsters.
Jumping and laughing and making a face,
    Many marvelous monsters.
They quickly bring smiles all over the place!
    Many marvelous monsters.
And when the monster time is through,
    Many marvelous monsters.
They return to the room as children like you!
    Many marvelous monsters.

☆Activities☆

This poem is about kids playing "pretend" in the dramatic play corner. Give children free reign to act like monsters during play time, and you may find they act less like monsters when you need them to behave! Encourage students to do the activities described in the poem: dressing up in hats, scarves, and "junk," making faces, pretend flying, doing magic tricks.

NO, NO NURSE!

by Ellen Booth Church

Have you heard the nutty news?
    No, no, nurse!

The doctor won't wear any shoes!
    No, no, nurse!

She wears her socks on her nose...
    No, no, nurse!

But not a stitch upon her toes!
    No, no, nurse!

☆ Activities ☆

* Create a classroom "Nutty News" paper—the sillier the better. It could include silly facts that children purposefully mix up and made-up gossip like the tale in the rhyme. Young kids love to make up absurd stories, and here is the place to put them all! Encourage children to use as many "n" words as they can in their reports. Photocopy the newspaper and send it home for families to enjoy!

* Ask: Have you ever heard of someone wearing a sock on his or her nose? Then make some funny sock noses in class. Provide recycled and art materials for children to make colorful, funny noses. Use pipe cleaners to make glasses onto which children can paste or tape their nutty noses.

ONLY OLD OKRA

by Ellen Booth Church

What can we find in the fridge to eat?
　　Only old okra!

We wanted cucumbers or some kind of meat.
　　Only old okra!

What can we do with this funny green stuff?
　　Only old okra!

Mix it with cat food and feed it to Puff.
　　Only old okra!

✰ Activities ✰

* Together, make a list of vegetables that are green. Bring in a few varieties and try them for snack. See which vegetables are the favorites.

* Delve into the concept of "old" vegetables! Leave a few varieties of vegetables on a plate for a few days and ask children to observe what happens to them. Provide magnifying glasses so that children can look closely at the decay and mold. Talk about mold and where it comes from. What color is it? Is it good to eat?

* Tell children you are going to have a "Mold Race" to see what food will grow mold the fastest! Set out three kinds of fruit and leave them (uncovered) on a windowsill. Each day, check to see which item has the most mold growing on it. Make a graph showing which piece gathers mold fastest.

PILES OF PURPLE PANCAKES

by Ellen Booth Church

Here's what we're having for breakfast today:
    Piles of purple pancakes!

With pineapple pizza and pumpkin paté!
    Piles of purple pancakes!

You bring the pretzels and pickled potatoes.
    Piles of purple pancakes!

And we'll have a picnic beneath the piano!
    Piles of purple pancakes!

☆Activities☆

✳ What a picnic this would be! Create an experience chart shaped like a picnic basket. Ask children to suggest all the "p" foods they can think of to take on the picnic—the grosser, the better! How many of these foods would the children actually eat?

✳ Make your own pile of purple (blueberry) pancakes to serve at snack time. Use an electric frying pan and make pancakes from a mix, adding frozen blueberries for color. Serve with purple syrup (blueberry or plum). Ask children to help brainstorm a purple juice to go with the meal.

QUICK QUIET QUAIL

by Ellen Booth Church

Did you see something queer go scurry by?
Quick quiet quail.

Without a sound or even a sigh,
Quick quiet quail.

By the quake of the feathers it must be a bird.
Quick quiet quail.

Yet it moves so quickly it can't be heard.
Quick quiet quail.

☆Activities☆

* What is a quail? Before showing pictures or giving hints, invite children to make predictions based on clues found in the rhyme. After they decide a quail is a bird, encourage children to describe what they think a quail looks like. Help them write or draw their ideas on an experience chart, then get out a book or photo card to compare students' predictions with the actual bird.

* Use Q-tips to paint quail pictures. Simply dip a clean cotton swab into paint (use a new swab for each color unless you want to combine colors). As children paint, have them imagine they are in the woods looking for quail. Where would they find one? Where would it hide?

RACING RED RACCOONS

by Ellen Booth Church

Riding up the hill, right there!
    Racing red raccoons!

Rounding to the corner, where?
    Racing red raccoons!

They go left, they go right.
    Racing red raccoons!

Now all are out of sight!
    Racing red raccoons!

☆ Activities ☆

* Keep the pace moving quickly when saying this rhyme so that it feels like a race. Repeat the rhyme over and over until the children are almost out of breath!

* Make "racing red raccoon" race cars out of cardboard boxes with wooden dowels and circle wheels. Decorate each with a distinctive design and have a race. Or have students race toy cars or balls and pretend they are raccoons.

* Use the rhyme to teach the concepts of "ght" and "left." When you reach the appropriate spots in the poem, extend your arm and point left, then right. Have children do the same.

"R" CHANT

Round and round the rugged rock
The ragged rascal ran.
How many R's are there in that?
Now tell me if you can!

☆Activities☆

✳ I think I was about eight before I stopped trying to count the "r's" and realized that there are no "r's" in "that." Little ones love the joke, but still enjoy counting all the "r's" they see and hear.

✳ Invite children to make up similar chants for other letters.

SEVEN SASSY SAILORS

by Ellen Booth Church

They set sail across the ocean blue,
    Seven sassy sailors!

They tried to trick me; they'll try to trick you!
    Seven sassy sailors!

Captain, send them back to shore!
    Seven sassy sailors!

Then they can't trick us anymore!
    Seven sassy sailors!

☆Activities☆

* Ask: What words that start with the "s" sound are in the rhyme? Have children circle all the words that start with "s" on the rhyme chart.

* What does "sassy" mean? Discuss the definition, then brainstorm other "s" adjectives that could be used in the poem.

* Create a regatta of "s" ships. Gather some foam s-shaped packing scraps (we sometimes call these "peanuts"). Glue these onto foam trays, which are available at little or no cost in the deli department of your local food market. Make handmade sails with paper and popsicle sticks or toothpicks. Finally, fill a sink and see if your ships are seaworthy!

TERRIBLE TEMPERED TEDDIES

by Ellen Booth Church

They're storming the hall and the nursery upstairs!
    Terrible tempered teddies!

Tearing up pictures and breaking up chairs!
    Terrible tempered teddies!

Now why would they want to behave that way?
    Terrible tempered teddies!

Oh, yes! We forgot their honey today!
    Terrible tempered teddies!

Activities

* Ask: What would a teddy bear look like when it was in a terrible temper? What do YOU look like when you are cross? Invite children to share their "mad" faces and to discuss what makes them feel upset or angry. What do they do when they feel a terrible temper coming on?

* Children can make teddy bear masks with paper plates or brown paper grocery bags. Provide plenty of art materials (felt, colored paper, buttons, etc.) for creating teddy bear ears and the vivid expressions on the teddy bear faces!

* Use an herbal (mint or chamomile) or decaffeinated tea for making "teddy tea." Serve it with honey for snack time.

UNDER UNCLE'S UMBRELLA

by Ellen Booth Church

What is the safest place in the rain?
Under uncle's umbrella.

We play in the water as it flows down the drain.
Under uncle's umbrella.

I always feel happy when we are together.
Under uncle's umbrella.

And when it stops raining, we'll dry off like a feather!
Under uncle's umbrella.

☆Activities☆

* Ask: Do you like to play in the rain? What do you do? Make an experience chart of all the things children like to do in the rain. Then invite them to add these activities to the rhyme.

* Bring a collection of old umbrellas out on the playground and use them to enact the rhyme. Don't forget to talk about safety rules first!

VERY VICIOUS VILLAINS

by Ellen Booth Church

They're stealing our vacation van!
   Very vicious villains!

And filling it full of vitamins!
   Very vicious villains!

This will stop them, a vacuum hose!
   Very vicious villains!

It will suck them up to their tippy toes!
   Very vicious villains!

☆Activities☆

* Ask: What is a villain? Do the characters in this rhyme seem like vicious villains or mischievous rascals? Talk about the difference and ask children to suggest other mischievous things for these funny villains to do with "v" objects—such as vegetables, vests, vinegar, vases, velvet, veterinarians, and violets.

* If you were going on a vacation in a van, what would you pack? Probably more than vitamins! Play this circle time game to explore the letter "v." Have the first person say one thing she would pack in the van. The next child says the first person's item plus his or her own. The next child says the other two plus his or her own. This pattern continues all the way around the circle and back to the first person, who must try to remember everything. This is a great listening and memory game to play with a small group of children!

WIGGLE WOOLLY WORM

by Ellen Booth Church

Watch that caterpillar go!
    Wiggle woolly worm!

Does it go fast? Does it go slow?
    Wiggle woolly worm!

Along hops a hungry robin now...
    Wiggle woolly worm!

Down a hole it goes with one last bow!
    Wiggle woolly worm!

☆Activities☆

* Help students investigate the difference between worms and caterpillars (sometimes called woolly worms). Compare appearance, habitat, and food. You will find information in books, encyclopedias, and on the Internet.

* Make caterpillar sock puppets to use for dramatization of the rhyme. Stuff cloth or newspaper in the sock toe to form the head. Use soft fabric and yarn scraps to create the fuzzy appearance and glue or sew on buttons for eyes.

A BOX FOR FOX SOCKS

by Ellen Booth Church

What is that strange box in the yard?
    A box for fox socks.

It's soft on the inside but the outside is hard.
    A box for fox socks.

It's filled with the most colorful warm things.
    A box for fox socks.

I wonder, if fox wear socks, can they wear rings?
    A box for fox socks.

Activities

* The letter "x" is a tough one to use in rhymes. This time, the alliterative letter is placed at the end of the word instead of the beginning. Ask children if they notice a difference between this poem and the others.

* Since the letter "x" is at the end of the word, it creates both a rhyme and an opportunity to work with a word family (-ox). Invite children to suggest other words for this family and add them to the rhyme. Point out that "socks" sounds like "fox" and "box," but has a different spelling.

* Use clean, old socks to make fox socks puppets. Don't forget the rings!

YUMMY YAM YOGURT

by Ellen Booth Church

Guess what we ate for dinner today?
    Yummy yam yogurt!

The same thing we ate yesterday.
    Yummy yam yogurt!

Yes, we never get tired of this yellow rubbish.
    Yummy yam yogurt!

We eat so much we look very tubbish!
    Yummy yam yogurt!

☆Activities☆

* What is a yam? Many young children are unfamiliar with this root vegetable. Bring one in for children to see, touch, cook, and taste. Make mashed yams sweetened with brown sugar or maple syrup. Then ask: Would this make good yogurt? If students feel adventurous, try mixing some sweetened cooked yams into vanilla yogurt.

* Ask: How many "y" words are in the rhyme? Invite children to suggest other words that start with the same letter sound. Add these to the rhyme. For example: A yak could yodel for more yogurt!

ZIP, ZAP, ZOOM!

by Ellen Booth Church

Did you see that zealous zebra go by?
　　Zip, zap, zoom!

He's gone to the zoo with a cherry pie!
　　Zip, zap, zoom!

It's Zelda the elephant's birthday today.
　　Zip, zap, zoom!

Go, zebra, go! The pie's getting away!
　　Zip, zap, zoom!

✧ Activities ✧

✳ Did you ever see so many "z" words in one rhyme? Have students count them! Ask: Do you know what all the words mean? Talk about the definitions of words like "zealous" (filled with enthusiasm). Do words like zip and zap have meanings? Can you make up other words that start with the letter sound of "z"?

✳ "Zip," "zap," and "zoom" are words that often appear in cartoon speech balloons as characters move through the action-packed strip. Invite children to cut pictures from comics and magazines with these or similar sound effects. Or, have children collaborate on their own comic strip illustrating the rhyme.

THE ALPHABET RHYME

A was an apple pie.
B bit it.
C cut it.
D dealt it.
E eats it.
F fought for it.
G got it.
H had it.
I inspected it.
J jumped for it.
K kept it.
L longed for it.
M mourned for it.
N nodded at it.
O opened it.
P peeped in it.
Q quartered it.
R ran for it.
S stole it.
T took it.
U upset it.
V viewed it.
W wanted it.
XYZ and ampersand.
All wished for a piece in hand.

☆Activities☆

Many children find it easiest to learn the alphabet by singing it. There are several tunes to try, and everyone knows the traditional alphabet song! This poem offers a new twist on learning the letters.

THE MINISTER'S CAT

The minister's cat is an angry cat called Alice.
The minister's cat is a beautiful cat called Bertie.
The minister's cat is a cuddly cat called Curly.
The minister's cat is a delightful cat called Daisy.
The minister's cat is an energetic cat called Earl.
The minister's cat is a fluffy cat called Furball.
The minister's cat is a great cat called Grant.
The minister's cat is a happy cat called Hazel.
The minister's cat is an ill cat called Icabod.
The minister's cat is a jolly cat called Jasper.

(and so on, through the alphabet...)

☆Activities☆

This rhyme works best when it's created by the students themselves.
Each person in the group takes a turn to make up a line about the
minister's cat that uses the appropriate letter of the alphabet. Students
love coming up with a descriptive word and a fun name for the kitty.

Counting Rhymes

Young children are often fascinated with organizing and numerating things; in fact, many youngsters surprise the adults around them by beginning to count on their own, with little or no instruction. Simple counting rhymes are a wonderful way to tap into children's natural enthusiasm for numbers. These rhymes make learning numbers play, not work. Children will take pride in being able to recount a rhyme and say the numbers in correct order (forward or backward, depending on the rhyme). They will enjoy the rhythm and language of the rhyme and beam as they realize that they are mastering an important basic skill.

Once children have mastered numbers, they have an important tool: They can communicate how old they are, how many cookies they want, even how long they had to wait for you! To help your students reach this point, recite and act out the counting rhymes frequently and enthusiastically. And whenever possible, provide manipulatives to make the activity concrete. Children will develop a better understanding of numbers if they can count their fingers, puppets, flannel board pieces, or any other objects that fit the rhyme.

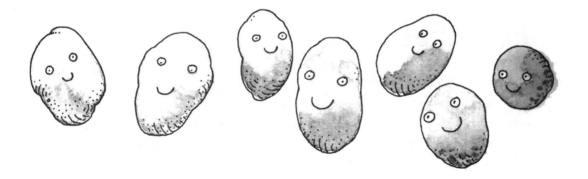

"You can not teach people anything, you can only help them discover it within themselves."
—Galileo

BEE HIVE

(Traditional)

Here is the bee hive, but where are the bees?
(Hand closed tight as hive)
Hidden away where nobody sees.
Watch and you'll see them come out of the hive.
1, 2, 3, 4, 5 !
(Hive opens, one finger at a time is extended. Then clap hands together as you pretend to catch one!)

☆ Activities ☆

* Set out a variety of materials for children (pipe cleaners, tape, glue, shimmery plastic, fabric, small pine cones, paper, glitter, etc.) and invite them to create their own bumble bees. Talk about what the bee might feel like: Would it be soft and velvety? hard and shiny? After children have created their bees, encourage them to attach their bees (with glue, tape, or pipe cleaners) to a hive. It could be a real abandoned hive you have discovered outside (make sure it is abandoned!) and brought into the classroom, or it could be a picture of a hive on the wall. Help children put their bees in groups of four or five and count their bees when they are all done!

FIVE LITTLE MONKEYS

(Traditional)

Five little monkeys sitting in a tree, *(Hold up five fingers.)*
Teasing Mr. Crocodile...
"You can't catch me!"

Along came Mr. Crocodile, quiet as can be.
SNAP! *(Snap your hands together.)*

Four little monkeys sitting in a tree, *(Hold up four fingers.)*
Teasing Mr. Crocodile...
"You can't catch me!"

Along came Mr. Crocodile, quiet as can be.
SNAP! *(Snap your hands together.)*

(Continue with numbers three through one, then recite:)

No little monkeys sitting in a tree, *(Hold up no fingers.)*
Teasing Mr. Crocodile...
"You can't catch me!"

☆ Activities ☆

* After you introduce this finger play and children are familiar with it, encourage them to act it out as a story with five children pretending to be monkeys and one as Mr. Crocodile. The more ways children can act out this scenario (with their fingers, then their bodies, then by drawing or even sculpting with play dough), the more they will become familiar with the numbers and counting concepts.

* Try doing the rhyme backwards. Start with one monkey, and have them come back out of the crocodile one at a time. Make the crocodile BURP instead of snap!

SING, SING, WHAT SHALL I SING?

Sing, sing, what shall I sing?
The cat's run away with the pudding bag string.
Do, do, what shall I do?
The cat has bitten it quite in two!

☆ Activities ☆

* You might have a room full of songwriters and not even know it! Use this familiar English nursery rhyme to lead you into some simple song writing while you practice counting. Use it when you are waiting for children to line up or while you are waiting to go outside or as a small group activity. Add your own last two lines for practice with counting like this:

  See, see, what do I see?
  The cat has bitten it quite in three!
  More, more, I see more.
  The cat has bitten it quite in four!
  Look, look! Perhaps it's alive!
  The cat has bitten it quite in five!
  And now from her famous bag of tricks,
  The cat has bitten it quite in six!
  Oh my goodness, it's going to heaven!
  The cat has bitten it quite in seven!

  (and so on as long as you feel like adding verses!)

* You can figure out your own new lines for the rhyme together with children. It doesn't matter a hoot if any of it really makes sense! The rhymes you use don't even need to be real words. Come up with the first line together with children, then ask one child to finish it with a number that rhymes with the last word.

* Invite children to be the cat and to cut their pudding bag string into as many pieces as they want. Provide scissors and string for each child. Then ask each child to cut the string and to count the number of pieces they end up with. You can also have children see which pieces are longest and which are shortest. Some children will be able to sequence the pieces by lining them up from shortest to longest.

ROLL OVER!

(Traditional)

There were five in a bed,
And the little one said, "Roll over! Roll over!"
So they all rolled over and one fell out.

There were four in the bed,
And the little one said, "Roll over! Roll over!"
So they all rolled over and one fell out.

Continue with numbers three and two, then move on to the last verse:

There was one in the bed,
And the little one said, "GOOD NIGHT!"

☆Activities☆

* Ask five children (fewer if you like) to lie down on the floor side by side as if they were in bed. Ask another child to put a blanket over the sleepers and tuck them all in. Then sing the song with the remaining children. On the "roll over" part of this song, invite everyone on the floor to "roll over" onto their tummies. Encourage the child on the very end to roll away from the group and "fall out" of bed. Continue this until all the children have "fallen" out of the bed, one at a time.

* You can vary this activity and provide children with choices by asking, "How else could the children fall out of bed besides rolling over?" Someone might suggest that they could fall out by laughing really hard! Then you can change the song to go something like this:
    *"So they all laughed hard
    And one fell out."*

* Keep asking for new things that the "little one said," and encourage children's imaginations. I once had a three-year-old offer the words, "Quit hogging the covers, you big oaf!" Everyone in my class sang: "Quit hogging! Quit hogging! So they all rolled over and one fell out..." What giggle-producing ideas will your children come up with?

ONE POTATO, TWO POTATO

(Traditional)

One potato, two potatoes,
Three potatoes, four,
Five potatoes, six potatoes,
Seven potatoes, more.

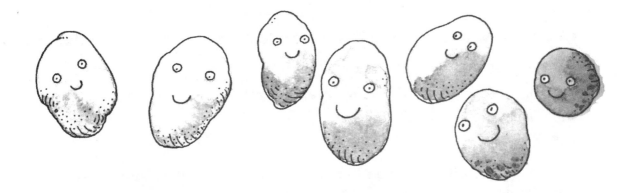

☆Activities☆

* This is a rhyme to decide who is going to be "it" in a game. Everyone puts their fists in front of them and someone counts the fists, going around in a circle. When the counter gets to "more," the person whose fist is touched puts the fist behind her back. The rhyme is said over and over until someone has both fists out of the ring OR until everyone has both fists out except one. Negotiating the rules is the best part!

* Learning to take turns and play fair are very important lessons. Talk about these issues in your class, and hang a list of "playing fair" rules generated by the children themselves.

EENIE, MEENIE, MINIE, MO

(Traditional)

Eenie, meenie, minie, mo
Catch a tiger by the toe
If he squeals,
Let him go,
Eenie, meenie, minie, mo.

☆Activities☆

There are many rhymes to eliminate players in a game, but this is one of the most famous. Nobody wants to be "mo!" After showing the children how to use the rhyme (see instructions for "One Potato," page 170), invite children to make up their own rhymes for counting turns. For the sake of simplicity, it is probably best to use a rhyme with ten words or beats. Have children clap out the ten beats, then make up nonsense words and phrases to match the beat. Try your original rhymes out the next time children are taking turns on outdoor play equipment.

TWO LITTLE DICKIE BIRDS

Two little dickie birds
Sat upon a wall.
Fly away, Peter.
Fly away, Paul.
Come back, Peter.
Come back, Paul.

☆Activities☆

* Put your fists together to represent the wall and hold up your forefingers as Peter and Paul. When they fly away, tuck them into your fist. Pop each one up as you call them back.

* Have two children act as Peter and Paul. When Peter flies away, ask how many birds are left. When Paul flies away, ask the question again. Reframe the answers so that the children begin to hear the kinds of questions and answers involved in beginning numeracy— if we take one away, one is left; take another one away and there are none left, etc.

* In movement class, have the children work in pairs as Peter and Paul. Have them find a place to be their wall. Get them to sit quietly for a few moments to think about where they might like to fly away to. What kind of birds are they? What are they going to see?

TEN GREEN BOTTLES

Ten green bottles hanging on the wall.
Ten green bottles hanging on the wall.
And if one green bottle should accidentally fall,
There'd be nine green bottles hanging on the wall.

Nine green bottles hanging on the wall.
Nine green bottles hanging on the wall.
And if one green bottle should accidentally fall,
There'd be eight green bottles hanging on the wall.

Eight green bottles hanging on the wall.
Eight green bottles hanging on the wall.
And if one green bottle should accidentally fall,
There'd be seven green bottles hanging on the wall.

(Continue with verses for numbers seven through zero.)

☆Activities☆

✳ If you are using this rhyme in a classroom, make ten cardboard bottles so that you can knock one down with each verse. Have the children count how many bottles are left.

✳ Make up your own version of this song using something the children know. For example, you could sing, "Ten school buses waiting in a line...And if one school bus should drive away in time..."

✳ Divide students into groups of ten (or fewer). Write the numbers 1 through 10 on cards and give each child a card. Tell them to use their numbers to stand in numerical order. Once the children are in their groups, they can call out their numbers in order.

ONE MAN WENT TO MOW

One man went to mow,
Went to mow a meadow.
One man and his dog
Went to mow a meadow.

Two men went to mow,
Went to mow a meadow.
Two men, one man, and his dog
Went to mow a meadow.

Three men went to mow,
Went to mow a meadow.
Three men, two men, one man, and his dog
Went to mow a meadow.

(Continue the verses, adding one more man with each verse until you run out of time or energy.)

☆Activities☆

* This is a tricky rhyme because it counts up and down at the same time. You'll get the best tongue-twisting, eye-crossing fun out of it if you chant it faster and faster as you go along.

* Act this one out. Have one child walk around with a stuffed dog while everyone sings the first verse. Have another child join him for the next verse, and so on. Call the children's attention to the idea of adding one. Keep asking: When you add one more, how many does that make? When you take one away, how many are left?

THIS OLD MAN

This old man, he played one,
He played nick nack on my drum.

CHORUS
(repeat after each verse):
With a nick nack paddy whack.
Give a dog a bone,
This old man came rolling home.

This old man, he played two,
He played nick nack on my shoe.

This old man, he played three,
He played nick nack on my knee.

This old man, he played four,
He played nick nack on my door.

This old man, he played five, He
played nick nack on my hive.

This old man, he played six,
He played nick nack on my sticks.

This old man, he played seven,
He played nick nack up to Heaven.

This old man, he played eight,
He played nick nack on my gate.

This old man, he played nine,
He played nick nack on my spine.

This old man, he played ten,
He played nick nack over again.

☆ Activities ☆

* This classic singing rhyme is a favorite with kids. The predictable quality of the rhyming words with the numbers often makes it one of the first songs that children memorize. Once children see the rhyming pattern, invite them to re-write the song with new rhyming words for each number. Ask: What else could this old man play ONE on (my thumb, bun, sun)? You will quickly see how well children are hearing the rhyming sounds.

* Get out your drums or coffee cans and tap out the rhythm of the song.

* As you begin each verse, you may wish to hold up the appropriate number of fingers to remind children which number you are on.

SIX LITTLE DUCKS

Six little ducks
That I once knew,
Short ones, tall ones,
Skinny ones too.
But the one little duck
With the feather in his back,
He led the others with a
Quack, Quack, Quack.
Quack, Quack, Quack.
Quack, Quack, Quack.
He led the others with a
Quack, Quack, Quack.

☆Activities☆

* Students will be fascinated to learn that male ducks really do have a feather sticking out of their backs. This is one way we can tell male ducks from female ones.

* This song tells how a male duck leads his friends into mischief and merriment. For an illustrated version of the story, see the book *Six Little Ducks* by Chris Conover (Thomas Y. Crowell Publishers).

* Create a new version of the song using everyone in the class. Do you have 18 children? Sing "18 Little Ducks" as children march around the room following one child who is holding the feather!

ONE, TWO, BUCKLE MY SHOE

One, two, buckle my shoe.
Three, four, shut the door.
Five, six, pick up sticks.
Seven, eight, lay them straight.
Nine, ten, a big fat hen!

☆Activities☆

✳ Have you ever wondered what this rhyme is about? Probably nothing!
It is just a fun way to remember the numbers. Say the rhyme with children and invite them to clap the rhythm as they say it. Do they hear a
pattern to the rhythm?

✳ What would happen if you add more numbers to the rhyme? Most
rhymes stop at ten but by nursery school and kindergarten, many children are ready to count much higher. Work together to create a second
verse to the rhyme using the numbers from 11 to 20, encouraging children to keep the rhyme and rhythm of the first verse.

FIVE LITTLE FISHIES
(A Fingerplay)

Five little fishies swimming in a pool.
(Wiggle five fingers.)
Th first one said, "The pool is cool."
(Show one finger while shivering.)
The second one said, "The pool is deep."
(Show two fingers and point downward with other hand)
The third one said, "I want to sleep."
(Show three fingers and pretend to sleep.)
The fourth one said, "Let's dive and dip."
(Show four fingers and move hand like a fish diving.)
The fifth one said, "I spy a ship."
(Show five fingers and pretend to look in the distance.)
The fisherman's boat comes,
(Put hands in a "v" shape to represent the front of the boat.)
The line goes splash,
(Pretend to throw in a fishing line.)
And away those five little fishies dash!
(Waggle fingers to show the fish swimming away.)

☆Activities☆

* This rhyme introduces ordinal numbers. Children learn early on what it means to be first but they rarely understand that second means the number 2, third means the number 3, and so on. Have 5 children act out the rhyme so they can make the connection between the cardinal and ordinal numbers. Line children in a row with each child holding a decorative paper fish with the appropriate numeral on it. Invite children first to recite the numbers on the fish, and then to say their placements in line as ordinal numbers.

ONE FINGER, ONE THUMB

(Tune: *Farmer in the Dell*)

One finger, one thumb, keep moving.
One finger, one thumb, keep moving.
One finger, one thumb, keep moving.
To chase the blues away.

One finger, one thumb, one hand, keep moving.
One finger, one thumb, one hand, keep moving.
One finger, one thumb, one hand, keep moving.
To chase the blues away.

Add a new body part with each verse:

One finger, one thumb, two hands...
One finger, one thumb, two hands, one arm...
One finger one thumb, two hands, two arms....
One finger, one thumb, two hands, two arms, one leg...
One finger, one thumb, two hands, two arms, two legs...
One finger, one thumb, two hands, two arms, two legs, one head...
One finger, one thumb, two hands, two arms, two legs, one head, one body...COLLAPSE!

☆Activities☆

* This song really gets kids moving and shaking! By the end of the song, they will be glad to collapse into a breathless pile on the floor—AND they will remember how to count how many hands, feet, legs, and arms they have!

* Invite children to use a mirror to count out and explore how many parts they have on their own bodies. Make an experience chart or graph of their findings. How many eyes do we each have? How many mouths? Check it out and then sing these body parts in the song too!

CINDERELLA DRESSED IN RED

(A Ball-Bouncing Rhyme)

Cinderella dressed in red,
What time did you go to bed?
1, 2, 3, 4, 5, 6, 7, 8, 9, 10, 11, 12.

Prince Charming dressed in red,
What time did you go to bed?
1, 2, 3, 4, 5, 6, 7, 8, 9, 10, 11, 12.

☆Activities☆

* This is a fun ball-bouncing rhyme. It challenges the player to bounce as long as he or she can without missing. Whatever number the player misses on is supposed to be the time he or she went to bed. Children think it is great fun to try to keep bouncing because they all want to stay up as late as possible!

* This type of bouncing game can be adapted to go with other numerical values. Children can make up a rhyme that counts up how much something costs, how old they are, or how many cookies they'd like to eat. For example:
    Puppy dog, puppy dog,
    How many dollars do you cost?
    1-2-3-4-5-6-7-8-9-10-11-12-13-14-15-16-17-18-19-20.

ONE, TWO, THREE, A-TWIRLSY

(A British Ball-Bouncing Rhyme)

One, two, three a-twirlsy,
Four, five, six, a-twirlsy,
Seven, eight, nine, a-twirlsy
Ten, a-twirlsy, CATCH ME!

☆Activities☆

✳ Stand children in a circle and give four of the children balls to bounce.
As they bounce, you and the other children will chant the rhyme.
When you get to the end of the rhyme, the children with the balls must
bounce the balls to someone new. Then you start the chant all over
again.

✳ Use the rhyme to start a game of tag. Have the child who is "it" stand in
the center of the gym or playground and recite the rhyme as he or she
twirls around. At the phrase, "catch me," the child runs and the others
try to tag him or her.

NUMBER ONE

Number one, touch your tongue.
Number two, touch your shoe.
Number three, scratch a flea.
Number four, touch the floor.
Number five, take a dive.
Number six, shake the mix.
Number seven, smile to heaven.
Number eight, through the gate.
Number nine, you're doing fine.
Number ten, do it over again!

☆Activities☆

* This is a great rhyme to get silly with. It gets even more exciting as you have the children say the rhyme over and over again, getting faster with each repeat. The end result is a bunch of giggling, tongue-tied children!

* This counting rhyme is perfect for depicting in a rebus chart. Write out each line using pictures for some of the words (shoe, door, etc.) and numerals for the numbers. This will make it easier for children to follow along as they say the rhyme.

CAUGHT A FISH ALIVE

(Sung Up and Down the Scale)

One, two, three, four, five,
I caught a fish alive.
Six, seven, eight, nine, ten.
I let him go again.

Why did you let him go?
Because he bit my finger so.
Which finger did he bite?
The little one on my right!

☆ Activities ☆

✳ This is a great counting rhyme to act out with your hands. Have children show fingers as they count and imitate the actions for each line of the rhyme (fishing, letting a fish go, etc.).

✳ What else might you catch if you went fishing? a shark? a crocodile? a boot? How would the rhyme be different with these other objects? Invite children to retell the rhyme with the new additions.

✳ Play a fish pond game. Ask children to draw, cut out, and decorate paper fish. Then add a paper clip to the mouth of each fish. Send children "fishing" in a pretend pond using dowels or sticks strung with magnets on the end of the line. When the magnet attracts a paper clip, the children will have a "catch."

FIVE LITTLE CHICKADEES

(Traditional)

Five little chickadees
Sitting on the floor.
One flew away,
And then there were four.

Chorus to repeat after each verse:

Chickadee, chickadee,
What do you say?
Chickadee, chickadee,
Fly away!

Four little chickadees
Sitting in a tree.
One flew away,
And then there were three.

Three little chickadees
Looking at you.
One flew away,
And then there were two.

Two little chickadees
Sitting in the sun.
One flew away,
And then there was one.

One little chickadee
Sitting all alone.
He flew away,
And then there were none.

☆Activities☆

* While sitting around a circle, choose five children to be the chickadees. They can take turns flying away during each chorus. The chickadees should move around the circle and come back to "roost" in their original spots.

* Practice subtraction with this chant. Have five children stand up as the chickadees. Ask: If there are five chickadees and one flies away, how many chickadees are left in the tree? If there are three chickadees and one flies away, how many are left? Use the children as "counters" to demonstrate the subtraction.

* Go to the library and look up chickadees. They are beautiful tiny birds with little black caps on their heads. Find out what types of seeds and foods they like and create a bird feeder for chickadees to hang outside the classroom window.

Science and Nature Rhymes

The natural world outside the school is a land of discovery for young children. The concepts, materials, and "magic" found in the outdoors are limitless and offer abundant opportunities for exploration.

Rhymes and chants are a wonderful way to begin your foray into this world. Use them to preface a theme unit or a nature walk—or as a way to recognize the natural world on a rainy or snowy day. In this section, you'll find rhymes about the sun, moon, and stars; the weather; the ocean; and more. Let these rhymes and chants lead you into the enchanting world awaiting you beyond the classroom doors.

"The real voyage of discovery consists not of seeking new landscapes but in having new eyes."
—Marcel Proust

MISTER MOON

Mister Moon, Mister Moon,
You're out too soon,
The sun is still in the sky.
Go back to bed and cover up your head,
And wait 'til the sun is nigh'.

☆Activities☆

✳ Perform this verse with exaggerated motions. It lends itself to children wagging a finger at the moon, covering their heads with their arms, and pretending to go to sleep. Try using it to calm children just before rest time.

✳ Props make this rhyme even more fun to enact. Create simple sun and moon masks with paper plates and popsicle sticks. Have children sit around in a circle, place a pillow and blanket in the center, and invite two children to use the masks. Have them start "rising in the sky" from opposite sides of the circle until the children sing "go back to bed!" Then, the moon snuggles up in the center for its nap and the sun travels across the sky to the other side of the circle.

✳ Did you ever notice that on some evenings you can see both the sun and the moon in the sky at the same time? This is fascinating to young children since most believe that only one can be in the sky at the same time. It is too early to teach much astronomy, but you can ask children where they think the sun and moon go when we can't see them in the sky. Children's answers will be enthralling!

TWINKLE, TWINKLE, LITTLE STAR

Twinkle, twinkle, little star,
How I wonder what you are.
Up above the world so high,
Like a diamond in the sky.
Twinkle, twinkle, little star,
How I wonder what you are.

☆Activities☆

＊ The person who wrote this rhyme thought the star looked like a diamond. Do the children know what a diamond is? What do *they* think the stars look like?

＊ Make splatter pictures of the night sky. First, give each child some dark blue or black paper to work with. Dip the bristles of an old toothbrush into white paint, then rub your thumb along the bristles so that tiny drops of paint fall onto the paper. To add a comet or meteor, put a larger drop of paint on the paper and use a straw to blow it in one direction, like a streak.

OLD WOMAN

There was an old woman tossed up in a basket
Seventeen times as high as the moon;
Where she was going, I couldn't but ask it,
For in her hand she carried a broom.
Old woman, old woman, old woman, quoth I,
Whither, O whither, O whither so high?
To brush the cobwebs off the sky!
Shall I go with you? Aye, by and by.

☆Activities☆

* In this rhyme, a woman travels into space in a basket in order to brush the "cobwebs" from the sky. Talk to the children about space travel in real life. Ask: How far could you get in a basket? How do astronauts get to the moon? After your discussion, draw spaceships. You can paste these onto the night sky pictures you made after singing "Twinkle, Twinkle" (see page 187).

* Have a countdown, just as NASA does when a shuttle launches into space. As a class, shout out: 10, 9, 8, 7, 6, 5, 4, 3, 2, 1, Blast Off! What a wonderful way to teach counting back from ten!

SKY RIDDLES

(Read the verses and have students guess at each object's identity.)

I am a ball of fire;
My jobs are heat and light.
I'm bringing some folks daytime,
While others have their night.
By day you'll always find me
Above you in the skies,
Though clouds may come between us
And hide me from your eyes.

(THE SUN)

I twinkle in the dark of night;
I have a million friends like me,
The sun in day makes so much light,
We are impossible to see.
In groups, we're constellations,
And sometimes given names.
Alone, some people choose us
To play their wishing games.

(THE STARS)

☆ Activities ☆

* These riddles can be tricky—but they sure are a lot of fun! Read each one aloud slowly so that children can absorb the clues. If they seem stumped, use hand motions to provide extra clues: For example, open and shut your hands repeatedly to show twinkling stars, or make a sunrise arch with your arms.

MORE SKY RIDDLES

(Read the verses and have students guess at each object's identity.)

Sometimes a circle, sometimes a half,
Sometimes a skinny crescent.
At night, a lot of people think
To gaze at me is pleasant,
I'm really round at anytime,
But circling the Earth,
I sometimes slip through shadows,
Which hide part of my girth.

(THE MOON)

The sun comes out to warm a rainy day,
And suddenly you see me in the sky!
My stripes of colors (seven every time),
Begin and end down low, but curve up high.

(A RAINBOW)

AIKEN DRUM

I knew a man lived on the moon,
Lived on the moon,
Lived on the moon.
I knew a man lived on the moon,
And his name was Aiken Drum.

And his hair was made of spaghetti,
Spaghetti,
Spaghetti.
And his hair was made of spaghetti,
And his name was Aiken Drum.

And his teeth were made of green cheese,
Green cheese,
Green cheese
And his teeth were made of green cheese,
And his name was Aiken Drum.

(Add other verses based on student input:)

And his eyes were made of...
And his toes were made of...
And his ears were made of...

Activities

* After you chant or sing this rhyme together, ask individual children to come up with their own choices as to what Aiken Drum is made of. Incorporate these ideas into the rhyme.

* If you have drums available in your classroom, hand them out to children and help them keep a steady beat to this song or chant. You can model loud and soft drumming. Be sure to come in hard on the word "Drum" at the end of the verse.

ONE MISTY MORNING

One misty, moisty morning,
When cloudy was the weather,
There I met an old man
Clothed all in leather.
I took him by the hand
And told him very plain,
How do you do? How do you do?
And how do you do again?

✫Activities✫

* Use this chant to talk about different ways of greeting people. Help children distinguish between appropriate ways to greet friends their own age and appropriate ways to greet others. Role-play greeting different people. For example, you might say, "Brian, you and your mom just saw your neighbor, Mrs. Clark, in the supermarket. Show me how you would greet her."

* This rhyme makes me think of those fairy tales when the bad sisters and brothers are cruel to some little old man or ugly creature, but the good sister or brother is kind and so is rewarded. When working on polite behavior, tell one of these stories and discuss what happens when we judge people by how they look.

WE'RE GOING ON A SPACE TRIP

We're going on a space trip.
All ready?
Let's go!
Put on your space suit.
Climb aboard.
Strap yourself in.
We're going on a space trip.
All ready?
Let's go!
10, 9, 8, 7, 6, 5, 4, 3, 2, 1...
Blast OFF!

Oh, look,
What's that?
It's the moon.
Can't go around it,
Can't go under it,
It's too far away!

Oh, look,
What's that?
It's a planet!
Can't go around it,
Can't go under it,
It's too far away!

**(Continue in this pattern
with verses about stars,
galaxies, the sun, etc.,
until students return to
Earth.)**

Activities

* This is a new version of the old favorite language game, "We're Going on a Bear Hunt." To play, children sit in a circle with the group leader. Children tap a steady beat on their legs as the chant is being recited. The leader says a line and the children repeat it, adding any appropriate hand motions. For example, students can act out putting on their space suits and blasting off.

IT'S RAINING, IT'S POURING

It's raining, it's pouring,
The old man is snoring;
He bumped his head,
When he went to bed,
And couldn't get up in the morning.

✩Activities✩

✱ Ask: How do you feel when it's raining outside? Do you ever feel like just going to bed? Divide students into two groups: those who like playing in the rain and those who do not like the rain.

STAR LIGHT, STAR BRIGHT

Star light, star bright,
First star I see tonight,
Wish I may, wish I might,
Have the wish I wish tonight.

✦ Activities ✦

✳ After you teach this rhyme, send home a note encouraging parents to take their children outside at nightfall to look for the first star of the evening. Have children sketch what they see using chalk or white crayon on dark-colored paper.

✳ Have students brainstorm other times we get to make wishes: blowing out the candles on a birthday cake, throwing a penny into a wishing well, etc.

✳ Encourage students to write their wishes on cut-out construction-paper stars. You can fasten these stars to one wall to create a wishing wall, or, to preserve students' privacy, let students take their stars home.

APRIL RAIN SONG

by Langston Hughes

Let the rain kiss you.
Let the rain beat upon your head
with silver liquid drops.
Let the rain sing you a lullaby.
The rain makes still pools on the sidewalk.
The rain makes running pools in the gutter.
The rain plays a little sleep-song on our roof at night—
And I love the rain.

☆Activities☆

* Tell this poem to children in an animated voice. Vary the pitch and the tone as you tell it. For example, whisper, "Let the rain kiss you," but raise your voice a little when you say, "Let the rain beat upon your head with silver liquid drops." Invite the children to chime in with the last line, "And I love the rain."

* After you have animated the poem in this way, ask children to think about what sounds they would make for rain "kissing" them. How do "silver liquid drops" sound when they land on their heads?

* Ask children to help you make up a rain lullaby. Would it be soft or loud? Fast or slow? Which instruments would they choose or not choose? What sounds could they make with just their hands or their own body? Would their lullabies have words or just sounds?

RAINING

A: It's raining and it's dripping
B: And the little trees are wet;
C: If one's a barrel-maker,
D: Inside a keg he'll get!
E: Inside a keg he'll get!
F: Inside a keg he'll get!
G: If one's a barrel-maker,
A: Inside a keg he'll get!

☆Activities☆

✱ Play a game called "Who's Missing" while you sing or chant this rhyme.
Ask all the children to get in a circle and place a large box or a blanket
in the center of the circle. As you sing the song ask everyone to close
their eyes. Then touch the head of one child who then goes "into the
keg" (in the box or under the blanket). When the song is over, ask the
other children to open their eyes and see if they can look around and
figure out who is inside the keg. Let the child who is under the box or
blanket pop out to surprise the others—whether or not everyone else
guesses right or not! This can be especially delightful for very young
kids (older two's or three's) who are just becoming aware of their
friends.

RAIN, RAIN, GO AWAY

Rain, rain, go away,
Come again another day.
All the children want to play.
Rain, rain, go to Spain,
Never show your face again!

☆Activities☆

* Use a world map to show students where Spain is located.

* Talk about the importance of rain for plants, animals, and people. Ask: Would we really want rain to go away forever? Why or why not? What are some ways we use water?

MY LADY WIND

My lady Wind, my lady Wind,
Went round about the house to find
A chink to get her foot in;
She tried the keyhole in the door;
She tried the crevice in the floor,
And drove the chimney soot in!

☆ Activities ☆

✳ This rhyme is a great lead-in to a discussion about wind. Ask children if they have ever seen the wind. Go on a hunt for the wind and see if you can find it outside! As you look, you can sing or chant this rhyme together. Ask children to find something that the wind has touched, and to put it in their pockets or hold it in their hands. Then ask them to find something the wind hasn't touched.

✳ Listen to the wind together, then make a list of all the sounds that the wind makes. You might even make up a song using all the sounds you come up with. Then ask children to move like the wind—when it is high in the pine trees, when it's coming through the keyhole or down the chimney, when it's blowing in an open field, when it turns into a tornado, when it goes to sleep, etc.

THE NORTH WIND

The North Wind doth blow
And we shall have snow,
And what will the robin do then, poor thing?
He'll sit in a barn
To keep himself warm,
And hide his head under his wing, poor thing.

☆Activities☆

* Discuss what animals do when winter comes. Collect books from the library that talk about winter camouflage, migration, and other seasonal adaptations. Use the information you uncover together to create new verses using new animals.

* Make a bird feeder for your classroom window. Be sure to keep it filled all winter long, because area birds will come to depend on it as a food source. Watch the birds feeding and keep a photo or illustration log of the feathered visitors.

THE BOTTOM OF THE SEA

A sailor went to sea, sea, sea
To see what he could see, see, see,
And all that he could see, see, see
Was the bottom of the deep blue sea, sea, sea.

☆ Activities ☆

✳ Make a classroom display of people and things at sea. Include pictures of different kinds of boats, sailors, fishermen, cars on a ferry, etc.

✳ Encourage children to pretend they are on a boat. Have them act out keeping their balance on deck, climbing ropes, throwing out nets, catching fish, fighting pirates, etc.

✳ Introduce older students to the simple homonym sea/see. Explain that these two words sound exactly alike, but have different spellings and different meanings.

Science

I SAW A SHIP

I saw a ship a-sailing
A-sailing on the sea
And, oh, but it was laden
With pretty things for thee.

There were comfits in the cabin
And apples in the hold.
The sails were made of finest silk
And the masts were made of gold.

The four and twenty sailors
That stood upon the deck
Were four and twenty white mice
With chains about their necks.

The captain was a duck
With a packet on his back
And when the ship began to sail,
The captain said "Quack, quack!"

☆Activities☆

* Have students draw pictures of what this glorious ship might look like, including its unusual crew.

* Recite the rhyme several times, changing the identity of the captain each time. This will enable you to teach and review the sounds different animals make. You might have a dog captain who says, "Woof, woof," or a pig captain who says, "Oink, oink." Let the children be the guides.

BOBBY SHAFTO

Bobby Shafto's gone to sea,
Silver buckles on his knee.
He'll come back and marry me,
Bonny Bobby Shafto.

Bobby Shafto's bright and fair,
Combing down his yellow hair.
He's my love for ever mair,
Bonny Bobby Shafto.

☆Activities☆

✳ Use a world map to show students all the places where a sailor could go to sea. Explain that on a map, blue represents water.

✳ Have students try singing the rhyme very fast; the last line of each verse is something of a tongue twister! Explain what a tongue twister is, then introduce others.

DANCE TO YOUR DADDY

Dance to your daddy,
My little laddie (or lassie),
Dance to your daddy
My little lamb.

You shall have a fishie
On a little dishie.
You shall have a haddock
When the boat comes in.

Activities

* The rhyme mentions one kind of fish the laddie's daddy might catch (haddock). Can your students name other kinds of fish?

* This poem is about a youngster waiting for his or her father to come home from fishing. Ask: Do you miss your mom or dad when he/she is at work? How do you make yourself feel better? How do you greet your parent when he or she comes home at night?

PUSSY WILLOW SONG

(Sung Up the Scale)

C: I know a little pussy
D: Whose coat is silver gray.
E: He lives down in the meadow,
F: Not very far away.
G: He'll always be a pussy,
A: He'll never be a cat,
B: Because he's a pussy willow!
C: Now, what do you think of that!

☆ Activities ☆

* When you teach this song to children, bring in pussy willows and pass them around. Ask children to touch the tips of the willows and see how soft they feel. If it's the dead of winter, you can make your own pussy willows with the children by using branches and (don't laugh!) dryer lint. Lint is cheap, easy to find, and easy to glue onto the end of the stick. You can also use gray felt, yarn, wool, or velour. Put them all in a vase after you are through and see how many different kinds of pussy willows children have created.

* If it is springtime and you live near a meadow, go there together and hunt for pussy willows. Or ask children to find some near their homes and bring them to school to share.

THE BUBBLE SONG

(Tune: *Sing a Song of Sixpence*)

Sing a song of bubbles
Floating in the air,
Filled with rainbow colors,
Swirling here and there.
Blowing lots of bubbles,
I don't want to stop.
What fun it is to catch one,
And touch it with a POP!

✩Activities✩

* Few objects fascinate children like bubbles. Why not invite children to pretend to be bubbles? Put on some soft background music to inspire children as they move through a hula hoop or large cardboard circle and come out as light and airy bubbles. You might say, "Oh, no, it's getting windy in here. How do bubbles move in the wind?" or "What happens when a bubble bumps into something?" They pop! "Popped" bubbles can go through the "wand" again to continue playing.

* Blow bubbles in your classroom, and help children look for all the colors of the rainbow. Later, have students describe the bubbles' properties (round, colorful, see-through, light, etc.) List their descriptions on chart paper.

UNDER THE SPREADING CHESTNUT TREE

Under the spreading chestnut tree,
With my banjo on my knee,
We're as happy as can be
Under the spreading chestnut tree!

☆Activities☆

* Invite children to move with this rhyme by making their bodies look like tall, spreading chestnut trees. Later, take the children outside to see how many different kinds of trees you can spot. You may wish to get a field guide and walk around for a while yourself before trying this with the children. That way, you will be able to identify at least some of the trees you see together.

* Invite a parent or friend to bring in a stringed instrument (a banjo or guitar will work well). Sing or chant the rhyme together with accompaniment. Vary the rhyme to include other trees, i.e.; "Under the spreading maple tree." Visit special trees outdoors and sing to them!

* While you're outside with children, or on another day, collect seeds and compare them with nuts you've brought into the classroom. Make a graph or chart with trees at the top and help children decide which seeds go with which trees.

Animal Rhymes

What is it about animals that children love so much? Young children feel a closeness to animals that comes from shared unconditional love and care. I believe that youngsters enjoy taking care of pets and other animals because the creatures are often smaller than they are. Think about it from a child's perspective: In a world where others take care of me and tell me what to do, it is empowering to have something of my own to love and care for!

You may use these rhymes to share the joy and humor of animals with the children. Some, like "Bat, Bat" (page 213), are simply goofy and fun; others, like "Little Pussy" (page 218), can be used to teach students the appropriate way to care for their animal friends.

"It often happens that a man is more humanely related to a cat or dog than to any human being"
— Henry David Thoreau

OVER THE HILL AND FAR AWAY

A: Over the hill to feed my sheep

B: Over the hill to Charley

C: Over the hill to feed my sheep

D: On buckwheat cakes and barley.

☆Activities☆

٭ See how many different tunes you can create together with children as you say this rhyme. Start by simply going up the scale with each line (as indicated with the lettered notes). Then experiment! For example, try playing or singing the first line and invite students to copy you using the same note.

٭ Use a small tape recorder to tape students' renditions of this tune, as well as new versions you come up with together.

٭ A wonderful extension activity for "Over the Hill and Far Away" is making pancakes. Buy real buckwheat flour to use in your recipe; it has a delicious and distinct taste. Make barley soup for lunch.

ANIMAL FAIR

(Minstrel Song)

I went to the Animal Fair.
The birds and the beasts were there,
And the old baboon by the light of the moon
Was combing his auburn hair.
The monkey bumped the skunk,
And sat on the elephant's trunk;
The elephant sneezed and fell to his knees,
And that was the end of the monk,
The monk, the monk, the monk,
The monk, the monk, the monk.

⭐Activities⭐

* Children love animals, and this is a perfect chant to teach them in preparation for going on a field trip to the zoo. Sing it on the bus on your way there and sing it again on your way home.

* Vary the last two lines by adding a new animal in place of the baboon: For instance, you could plug in "the great big bear with the chocolate brown hair." Then ask children, "What was the bear doing?" When a child pipes up, "Was giving us silly stares" (or some other fun response), incorporate these words into the last line. Then start the rhyme all over again and add a new animal you have seen at the zoo. It doesn't matter a bit if anything rhymes! This is a fun way for children to remember and think about the animals they have just seen.

BLUE

(tune: *Twinkle, Twinkle Little Star*)

I had a dog and his name was Blue
Betcha five dollars he's a good dog too!

Here, Blue! You good dog, you!
Here, Blue! You good dog, you!

He showed me a hole in the crack of the fence
Where the hog went through for a mere three pence!

Here Blue! You good dog, you!
Here Blue! You good dog, you!

☆Activities☆

* Host a "Pet Party" in your classroom and share this rhyme with children as you prepare for it. Talk about different kinds of dogs and cats and what they like to eat, how they play, how they show happiness and sadness, and what they like to chase. For the "Pet Party," ask each child to bring in photos of his or her pet; a lock of its hair; a paw print made with parents at home; or even, if you are set up for it, the actual pet (one pet at a time of course!). Because children are so attached to and proud of their pets, this type of party will boost the self esteem of the pet owner. It will also increase children's respect for animals.

* Ask your local veterinarian for free or inexpensive posters of different dog and cat breeds. See if children can identify their own pet breeds.

* Extend this activity by inviting a veterinarian to come into your school and share how she or he helps animals.

BAT, BAT

Bat, bat, come under my hat
And I'll give you a slice of bacon;
And when I bake,
I'll give you a cake,
If I am not mistaken!

✬Activities✬

✳ Use this rhyme to lead in to a discussion about bats. Read about bats in *Ranger Rick* magazine or *Zoo Books*. Then ask children if they think bats really would eat a slice of bacon or a cake. Make a list of all the things children think bats will eat and all the things bats won't eat. Then make a list of what humans eat and compare lists.

✳ Since bats love berries, you might extend this bat theme by going on a field trip to pick berries and then making "Bat Jam" with children!

✳ Share these bat facts with your class:
— Bats are mammals, just like dogs, cats, cows, and people.
— But unlike other mammals, they can fly!
— There are more than 850 different kinds of bats.
— Most bats look for food at night and sleep during the day.

FIVE LITTLE DUCKS

Five little ducks went swimming one day
Over the pond and far away.
The mother duck said,
"Quack, quack, quack, quack, quack!"
But only four little ducks came back.

Four little ducks went swimming one day
Over the pond and far away.
The mother duck said,
"Quack, quack, quack, quack!"
But only three little ducks came back.

(Repeat the above stanza with numbers three, two, and one, before moving on to the final stanza:)

No little ducks went swimming one day
Over the pond and far away.
The mother duck said,
"Quack, quack, quack, quack, quack."
(Loudly) Then five little ducks came swimming back!

☆Activities☆

* Invite groups of six students to act out the rhyme on the playground or in the gymnasium.
* This rhyme can be used to teach the numbers zero through five, including counting these numbers backward. Write the numbers on the board before you begin the rhyme. If students need a gentle reminder at the start of each stanza to remember how many ducks went swimming and how many came back, point to the appropriate number with a yardstick and challenge students to name the number themselves.

TEENSY, WEENSY SPIDER

The teensy, weensy spider
Climbed up the water spout.
Down came the rain
And washed the spider out.
Then out came the sunshine
And dried up all the rain.
And the teensy, weensy spider
Climbed back up again.

☆Activities☆

✳ There are several slightly different versions of this rhyme. For example, in one, the spider is the "itsy, bitsy spider." Ask students if they have sung different versions and invite them to share their versions with the class.

✳ Teach students the classic hand motions to go with this rhyme. Touch the thumb of one hand to the forefinger of the other, then rotate them, making your hands look like a climbing spider. When it rains, wiggle your fingers to show the downpour. When the sun shines, make a sunrise motion with your hands.

✳ To demonstrate how the sun could dry up all the rain (the concept of evaporation), place a saucer of water on a sunlit window sill. Ask students to predict what will happen to the water, then watch for several days as the water level shrinks.

ELEPHANTS CAME OUT TO PLAY

One elephant came out to play
Upon a spider's web one day.
It was such enormous fun
That he called for another elephant to come.

Two elephants came out to play
Upon a spider's web one day.
It was such enormous fun
That he called for another elephant to come.

**(Continue to number ten or higher, then
move on to the final stanza:)**

Ten elephants came out to play
Upon a spider's web one day.
It was such enormous fun,
But bedtime came, and they were done.

Activities

* Help children glue some string onto a card to make a spider-web pattern.

* Stand children in a circle and have everyone hold onto a sheet or table cloth. As children say the rhyme, put soft stuffed toys onto the middle of the sheet and bounce them up and down (as if they were the elephants at play). Use light, medium-weight, and heavy toys, and ask children to observe how the different toys move on the sheet.

PUSSY CAT, PUSSY CAT

Pussy cat, pussy cat, where have you been?
I've been to London to visit the Queen.
Pussy cat, pussy cat what did you there?
I frightened a little mouse under her chair.

☆Activities☆

✳ Discuss as a class: Who has a cat? Does the cat go outside or stay in the house? Where do students think the cat goes when it goes out (or where does the cat dream of going)? Does the cat have secret adventures like the cat in this rhyme?

✳ Have students rewrite the last line of the poem, using words that rhyme with "there."

LITTLE PUSSY

by Jane Taylor

I love little pussy.
Her coat is so warm.
And if I don't hurt her,
She'll do me no harm.
I won't pull her tail
Or chase her away.
Little pussy and I
Very gently will play.
I'll sit by the fire,
And give her some food,
And pussy will love me,
Because I am good.

☆Activities☆

* Discuss: How do you look after a cat? What do cats like to eat and drink? What games do they like to play? Is it important to be gentle with animals? Why?

* Pretend to be a cat. Go out on the prowl. Check out the neighborhood. Come home and have a good wash, then stretch out for a long sleep in a warm place.

* Look at a picture of a cat and discuss the whiskers, the ears, and the tail. What are they for? How are they the same as other animals' whiskers, coats, and tails? How are they different?

HARK, HARK

Hark, hark, the dogs do bark.
Beggars are coming to town,
Some in rags
And some in tags
And one in a velvet gown.
Some gave them white bread
And some gave them brown
And some said they should be whipped
And ran them out of town.

☆Activities☆

✳ Ask children to describe what a watch dog does and what types of dogs make good watch dogs.

✳ Some children are afraid of dogs, especially when they bark. It is very sensible to be careful of strange dogs and it is important not to make fun of children's fears. However, you may want to invite students who are not afraid of dogs to talk about good ways to get to know a friendly dog. What do dogs like? How do dogs behave when they are trying to get to know a new person?

A BIRD CAME DOWN

(An Excerpt)

by Emily Dickinson

A bird came down the walk
He did not know I saw;
He bit an angleworm in halves
and ate the fellow raw.

And then he drank a dew
From a convenient grass,
And then hopped sidewise to the wall
To let a beetle pass.

☆Activities☆

✳ As children recite this beautiful rhyme, use handmade puppets to act out the scene. Students can make simple puppets with paper bags or clean socks. You can also use props to represent each "character" (a pipe cleaner for the worm, a feather for the bird, etc.).

✳ Use the poem as a springboard for heading outdoors. Take a class walk around your school or neighborhood, looking for birds, worms, beetles or other bugs, and grass wet with dew.

✳ At snacktime, serve cups of "dew" (juice or water).

✳ Extend the activity by asking children to substitute new animals in the rhyme:

> *A HORSE flew in the sky.*
> *He did not know I saw;*
> *He bit the MOON in half*
> *And ate the fellow raw.*

Time Rhymes
(Hours, Days, Months, Seasons)

The concept of time can be a difficult one for children to grasp. Children tend to live in the present moment, so the concept of "yesterday," "today," and "tomorrow" can seem irrelevant to them! Yet the ways of the world require children to learn about time, days, months, and seasons. The rhymes in this section help children learn a little about them in a fun, playful format. The children will learn that there is such a thing as time; and that time is measured by the clock, by the season, and many other ways.

You may want to use a large paper or cardboard clock to show the times mentioned in the rhymes as you say them. In addition, you might want to create a classroom "time line" to show the events of each day. Invite children to help take photos of each of the special events of the day (arrival, circle time, centers, snack, etc.). Attach these to cardboard and add a picture of a clock showing the appropriate time of the day for the activity. Hang the cards in order, from left to right, in a place where children can refer to the photos and times. By connecting the idea of time to something that is meaningful to them, you help them to see the purpose and usefulness of understanding time.

And, of course, sing about time as often as you can! Keep in mind that before children can learn to *tell* time, they need to be aware *of* time. Using repetitive rhymes to play with the ideas of time is a great place to start!

**"Who forces time is pushed back by time;
who yields to time finds time on his side."
—The Talmud**

THE MOUSE AND THE CLOCK

Hickory, dickory, dock!
The mouse ran up the clock;
The clock struck one,
And down he run,
Hickory, dickory, dock!

✩ Activities ✩

* Ask children to describe the clock in the rhyme. Most children will conjure up a tall grandfather clock, since these clocks chime on the hour. However, encourage students to be creative and to name as many different kinds of clocks as they can.

* Use the poem to explain that one o'clock could be very early in the morning or in the early afternoon, just after lunch. Show what one o'clock looks like on a clock or watch.

* Lead the class in a discussion of the regular events in its school day. Ask: What do we do in the morning? In the afternoon? Do you know what we are doing at one o'clock in the afternoon? What about one o'clock in the morning (in the middle of the night)? Who is here at school at that hour? Be prepared for some interesting answers and discussions!

* What would happen if the clock struck two? Invite children to write new verses for the rhyme using each hour. For example: "The clock struck two and he lost his shoe, Hickory, Dickory, Dock!" or "The clock struck three and he bumped his knee, Ouchery, Ouchery, Dock!"

ELSIE MARLEY

Elsie Marley is grown so fine,
She won't get up to feed the swine,
But lies in bed till eight or nine.
Lazy Elsie Marley.

☆Activities☆

* Do the children know what time they wake up in the morning? Who awakens first in their house? Who likes to get up? Who likes to stay in bed? Have a lively discussion about everyone's wake-up habits.

* Ask: What are some reasons we can't stay in bed as long as we may want to? (school, work, etc.)

BEDTIME PROVERB

Early to bed,
Early to rise
Makes a man healthy,
Wealthy, and wise.

☆Activities☆

✳ This is a proverb, or wise saying. Ask the children if they think the proverb is true: Does going to bed early help a person stay healthy? Does it make them smarter or richer?

✳ Talk to the children about how it feels to be tired. Ask: Who has a baby brother or sister who is very crabby when he or she needs a nap?

WEE WILLIE WINKIE

Wee Willie Winkie
Runs through the town,
Upstairs, downstairs
In his night gown.
Tapping at the windows,
Crying through the lock,
Are all the children in their beds?
It's past eight o'clock.

 ## Activities

* Have a class discussion about bedtimes. Do the children know what time they go to bed? Do they have the same bedtime every night, or does it change on the weekend?

* Ask: What do you have to do to get ready for bed? Have children illustrate their bedtime routines on separate index cards. Then have the children shuffle the cards and try to put them back in the proper sequence.

A DILLER, A DOLLAR

A diller, a dollar,
A ten o'clock scholar,
What makes you come so soon?
You used to come at ten o'clock
But now you come at noon.

☆Activities☆

* Talk about the importance of being on time. Ask: When do you have to be on time? What can children do to help arrive on time? Discuss planning ahead, getting ready for school in the morning, and having a good night's sleep.

* Show students the difference between ten o'clock and noon on a cardboard clock. Explain that the scholar in the rhyme was two hours late for his or her studies. To help students conceptualize this amount of time, set a timer for two hours.

WHAT'S THE TIME, MR. WOLF?

(A Chanting Game)

One person is chosen to be Mr. Wolf. He or she stands alone in front of the class, with everyone else facing the opposite wall.

Everyone chants:
> "What's the time, Mr. Wolf?"

Mr. Wolf turns back to them and says,
> "One o'clock."

Mr. Wolf moves forward a step or two. Everyone else moves forward a little and chants again:
> "What's the time, Mr. Wolf?"

Mr. Wolf turns back and says,
> "Two o'clock," and so on through the hours.

When he feels like it, Mr. Wolf can turn back and answer,
> "Dinner time!"

Then Mr. Wolf runs to catch someone if he can. That person then becomes Mr. Wolf!

☆Activities☆

* Play this chanting game in the gym, on the playground, or someplace else where you have a lot of space for running around. If you find that the same few students are always Mr. Wolf, assign a new child to be Mr. Wolf every once in a while; no child should miss out on the recitation of the time!

* Talk about wolves in fairy tales. Ask: Why are wolves always the bad guys? Have students name other games and stories in which wolves are the villains.

MONDAY'S CHILD

Monday's child is fair of face,
Tuesday's child is full of grace,
Wednesday's child is full of woe,
Thursday's child has far to go,
Friday's child is loving and giving,
Saturday's child works hard for its living,
But the child that is born on the Sabbath day
Is bonny and blithe and good and gay.

☆Activities☆

* This is the original British rhyme; you may wish to change the description for Wednesday's child to something more flattering, perhaps, "Wednesday's child is in the know," or "Wednesday's child goes with the flow." Invite students to ask their parents on what day of the week they were born, and help each child find his or her description in the rhyme.

* Explain that the Sabbath day in this poem is Sunday. Then help students copy the seven days of the week from the poem and write them on chart paper. Recite them aloud over and over until students get them straight.

SOLOMON GRUNDY

Solomon Grundy
Born on Monday,
Christened on Tuesday,
Married on Wednesday,
Took ill on Thursday,
Worse on Friday,
Died on Saturday,
Buried on Sunday,
And that was the end of Solomon Grundy.

* To learn the days of the week, children have to hear them chanted as a list as often as possible. This poem may seem morbid, but I have found that children find it really funny. One way to enjoy the rhyme together is for you to read the first part of each line, leaving off the day of the week. Have students chime in with the day. Soon they will be able to say the days in order, even without the rhyme.

* When children are getting good at saying the days of the week, try starting with a different day each time they practice. This will help cement the list in the children's minds and help them to see the circular pattern.

* Make a wall chart showing the day, the date, the month, and the year. Every day, change the relevant parts and ask: What day is it today? What do we do on (Mondays)? Do we come to school tomorrow? What day was it yesterday?

* Discuss the children's weekly routine: How many days are there in a week? Which days are school days? Which days make up the weekend? What day of the week do the children like best? Why?

THE MONTH RHYME

Thirty days has September,
April, June, and November.
All the rest have thirty-one,
Except February alone,
Which has twenty-eight days clear
And twenty-nine in each leap year!

☆Activities☆

✳ Make a wall display with the children. Write the months of the year in a list and beside each one put pictures of events which happen that month—a pumpkin for Halloween, a Christmas tree or Hanukkah menorah, etc.

✳ Make a picture graph of the months that have 30, 31 and 28 (29) days! Because the idea that months have different numbers of days is probably new to children, back up your graph with a look at a real calendar.

Silly Rhymes

Children are among the greatest laughers on the planet, so rhymes and chants that tickle funny bones are often the most favored ones of all. The rhymes in this section will help children discover their own senses of humor. It is a valuable discovery because the ability to find humor and delight in different situations enhances a child's social interactions throughout life. Silliness and laughter pay dividends every day in your classroom. By releasing endorphins in the body, laughter creates a natural sense of euphoria in both children and adults.

You can foster humor in your classroom by providing an atmosphere where children feel safe enough emotionally to "cut loose" once in a while (or more than once in a while). That means you should be willing to set aside your own inhibitions. This may be your most difficult task as a teacher, but it is very important. Let children see who you are, and what truly strikes you funny! Let them see you laugh loud and long and often!

In addition to enjoying silly rhymes together, share plenty of simple jokes in your classroom. Keep in mind that children don't necessarily need to understand the punch line in order to appreciate the joke. They'll often laugh hardest at something that makes NO SENSE at all and take delight in retelling it their own way. It's important that children have opportunities to do this without being "judged" by both adults and peers. Nothing empowers a child like making someone else laugh!

Remind students that humor should always be tasteful and respectful. Students must avoid name calling, ethnic slurs, and other remarks that may hurt others. In other words, emphasize that humor should be all in "good" fun.

As children "play" with words, rhymes, chants, jokes, and silly stories, they will become aware of the joy of "making fun" in a healthy way, not at the expense of others. So start early and have fun with these silly rhymes and songs. It will make everyone feel better!

**"The next best thing to solving a problem
is finding the humor in it."
— Frank A. Clark**

LAZY MARY

Lazy old Mary, will you get up,
Will you get up today?
Lazy old Mary, will you get up,
Will you get up today?

What will you give me for breakfast
If I get up today?
A slice of bread and a cup of tea
If you'll get up today.

☆Activities☆

✳ Sing this rhyme once in a while at snack time or at breakfast time if
you have one. After children become familiar with it, ask them to use
their imaginations to describe what else they could have for breakfast.
Model some silly answers: "Some pickle juice and half a raisin!" or
"Two fried minnows and eight rotten olives if you'll get up today!"

✳ You can make a good movement game out of this rhyme by inviting one
child to be Lazy Mary. Have her lie down with her eyes closed in the
center of the circle while others sing the rhyme. When the class reaches
the line, "Will you get up today?" Mary refuses. She finally gets up
when she is offered her favorite food for breakfast. Let children in the
circle take turns thinking of something to offer Lazy Mary!

WHOOPS, JOHNNY

Johnny, Johnny, Johnny, Johnny,
Whoops Johnny,
Whoops Johnny,
Johnny, Johnny, Johnny!

✿Activities✿

✳ This is a simple little chant but it can be the start of a lot of silly movement and fun. It can be especially delightful for 3-year-olds, who are enchanted with simple surprise twists! Start by holding up a child's hand and touching each fingertip on the first four "Johnny's." Then, on the word, "whoops," slide down the index finger. Touch the tip of the thumb on the next "Johnny" and pop back up again on "whoops." Finally, repeat the process backwards on the last four words of the rhyme. After you show children how to do this, let them do it for themselves as you sing the chant together. When they are comfortable with this, ask children to find partners and perform the finger play on their friends' hands. Then switch, so the other children have turns.

✳ Invite two children to hold hands and make a bridge for other children to walk under. On the word "whoops," the two children collapse the bridge around whomever is underneath. That child gets to pick a partner and make the next bridge. Ask children how else you could move while you sing this rhyme. They'll come up with great ideas!

WE'VE BEEN WORKING ON OUR BUILDINGS

(Tune: *I've Been Working on the Railroad*)

We've been working on our buildings
All the preschool *(or kindergarten or school)* day.
We've been working on our buildings,
The time just slipped away.
Can't you hear the tools singing?
"Look what we made today!"
Can't you hear us saying,
"Let's go out and play!"? *(or "Hip, Hip and Hooray!")*

☆Activities☆

✳ Sing this when its time to clean up the building blocks or other toys. It's a neat way to recognize the fabulous towers and bridges the children have labored over.

✳ You can easily change the words to this rhyme to reflect other activities the children have been involved in. You might sing, " We've been painting our pictures," or "We've been hearing stories." What else have the kids been working on today in class? Let them tell you!

OLD DAN TUCKER

Get out of the way for old Dan Tucker.
He's come too late to get his supper.
Supper's over and breakfast's cooking.
Old Dan Tucker's standing looking.

☆Activities☆

* This fast-paced rhyme is simply delightful to chant together with a great rhythmic cadence. It can be a great transitional rhyme for lining up for the bathroom, brushing teeth, or waiting for mealtime.

* Substitute children's names for "Old Dan Tucker," and watch children's faces light up as they hear their own names.

DICKERY, DICKERY, DARE

Dickery, dickery, dare
The pig flew up in the air!
The man in brown soon brought him down.
Dickery, dickery, dare.

☆Activities☆

* What a silly rhyme! Pigs flying through the air and men in brown bringing them down! Ask children if they've ever seen a pig fly. What else could fly through the sky? Let the children have fun coming up with animals they would like the man in brown to bring down. For example:

    Dickery, dickery, dare
    The cow flew up in the air!
    The man in brown soon brought her down.
    Dickery, Dickery, Dare.

* Add as many unlikely flying animals as you can think of...baboons, hippos, elephants, whales, buffalo, crocodiles! Children will take great delight in these images of flying animals!

* Go on from animals to other categories of identified "flying objects!" Vehicles, furniture, food, and so on can fly through the air. Encourage children to let their own creative imaginations fly.

* Make a mural together of all the animals or other objects the man in brown has brought down today. You can also make a huge collage by cutting out pictures from magazines. If you are looking for a challenge, help children create a mobile of all the animals they have thought of.

THE SQUIRREL WENT OUT TO CUT THE HAY

The squirrel went out to cut the hay;
Did you hear how he chattered and chattered away?
The blackbird raked, the crow pulled the load
And pussy-cat drove the cart way down the road!

☆Activities☆

✳ Ask children to listen very carefully to the song as you sing it, and ask them to lift up a finger every time they hear an animal in the song. After you have repeated this activity with children several times (you can do it while they wait for the bathroom, or even outdoors in a small group), ask them to find a partner and hold both hands. Ask them to lift up their hands together every time they hear an animal mentioned in the song. This will be easier and easier as they become more familiar with the song. Then ask them to find a third partner and all hold hands. Repeat this until everyone is united in a circle.

✳ You can vary the actions for this rhyme by designating a few children to be the squirrels and a few to be the crows, the pussy cats, and the blackbirds. Ask them to "chatter," "rake," "pull their load," or "drive the cart" as the case may be when they hear their animals mentioned in the song. Be sure to sing or say the rhyme very slowly at first to give kids time to catch on!

THERE'S A HOLE IN THE BUCKET

There's a hole in the bucket, dear Liza, dear Liza.
There's a hole in the bucket, dear Liza, there's a hole.
Then fix it, dear Henry, dear Henry, dear Henry.
Then fix it, dear Henry, dear Henry, then fix it.

With what shall I fix it, dear Liza, dear Liza?
With what shall I fix it, dear Liza, with what?
With some straw, dear Henry, dear Henry, dear Henry.
With straw, dear Henry, dear Henry with straw!

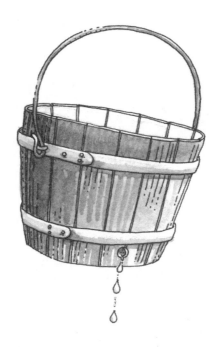

☆Activities☆

What a great opportunity to foster problem-solving skills! Ask: How could Henry and Liza fix their bucket (besides using straw)? Incorporate students' ideas into the rhyme.

DOT'S DINER

by Deb Hensley

Here's what's on the menu at Dot's Diner down to town.
Dot does all the cooking, bring your fork and come on down.
Such a grand selection you have never seen before.
This will fill your gullet till you're begging for some more:
Greasy goopy gravy that goes gummy on your spoon,
And then it all coagulates like glue until you swoon!
Peanut butter pickles that will stand your hair on end;
Dip them in some fish eggs as you share them with a friend!
Fresh desserts of cow pies more delicious than a dream,
They're really very tasty and they're best enjoyed with cream.

⭐Activities⭐

* Create a restaurant/diner theme in your dramatic play area today! Add hats that say "Dot's Diner," aprons, order pads, and pencils. Try to find a variety of "real" restaurant props: printed place mats, napkin holders, real flatware, ketchup bottles, etc. Then share this song with the children and get the sillies flowing! Add some pizzazz to your theme by brainstorming "gross-out" foods with children! See who can think up the grossest or silliest food.

TIMOTHY WINK

By Deb Hensley

What shall we do about Timothy Wink?
He's gotten so small he might slip down the sink.
He never eats breakfast or lunch anymore.
He's gotten so small he might melt to the floor.

What shall we do about Timothy Wink?
We've tried all the regular things we can think.
So he'll eat up his supper and sip on his drink.
Won't you help us to fatten up Timothy Wink?

✰Activities✰

✳ Ask: How could you fatten up Timothy Wink? Ask children to think of really tasty foods that would help Timothy grow strong and healthy. Provide magazines for children to browse through and cut out pictures to make a collage of foods. Set out cookbooks with pictures and help children pick out good things for Timothy to eat.

✳ Make a nutritious snack together for the "invisible" Timothy Wink. As you eat the snack, ask children to be looking around the room for him. Remind students, "He's very tiny, so keep an eye out!" You can suggest that children leave a little plate of the nutritious snack out on the table for Timothy. Maybe he'll sample the goodies after everyone else has gone home.

GINNY PECKINPAUGH

By Deb Hensley

My best friend Ginny Peckinpaugh
Likes graham crackers and milk.
She dips them in her cup and then
She giggles as they wilt.
We chortle when they wiggle
And they turn to liquid slop,
And laugh until we're snorting
As the graham crackers go PLOP!

☆Activities☆

* Have graham crackers for snack today. Show children how they can dunk their crackers in their milk as you share this rhyme with them. (Make sure they know it's important not to get so silly that the milk spills.)

* Make a pie with a graham cracker crust and show children how to grind the crackers up with a rolling pin. Spread cream cheese on graham crackers at lunch time.

* Take teddy bears or other "animals" on a graham cracker picnic outside!

I KNOW A POOR PELICAN

(Tune: *I Know An Old Lady*)

by Ellen Booth Church

I know a poor pelican who swallowed a pie.
I don't know why he swallowed the pie.
Perhaps he'll die.

I know a poor pelican who swallowed a pig,
I don't know why he swallowed the pig.
He swallowed the pig to catch the pie.
I don't know why, he swallowed the pie.
Perhaps he'll die.

Activities

* Keep adding on to this cumulative song, making the poor pelican eat more and more foods. Each time you start a new verse, point to a child and let him or her name the next item on poor pelican's menu. Be sure to keep it in the "p" family!

* Change the letter, and you have a whole new song. Instead of singing about the poor pelican, you might choose a lazy lion or a blind bat. Then make sure the creature eats only foods that start with the same initial letter.

MY HAT IT HAS THREE CORNERS

My hat it has three corners,
Three corners has my hat;
And had it not three corners,
It would not be my hat!

☆ Activities ☆

✳ Here is a fun rhyme that incorporates both numbers and geometric concepts. Introduce it by singing it aloud (you can make up your own tune!) and wearing your own newspaper hat with three corners. Talk about the points and angles in a corner and what a corner looks like. Show children how you made your three-cornered hat.

✳ During large or small group time, ask children to look for corners throughout the room. Let them go on a "corner hunt." Invite them to find as many corners in the room as they can (boxes, shelves, ceiling corners, wall corners, chair corners) Provide them with stickers to "label" the corners. Don't forget about the ceiling!

✳ Provide paper for children to make their own three-cornered hats. All the hats will look different, of course. Help children count the corners they have made in their hats. Some may have a lot more than three!

WHAT DID YOU SAY?

The man in the wilderness asked of me,
How many strawberries grow in the sea?
I answered him as I thought good,
As many red herrings as grow in the wood.

☆Activities☆

✴ Here is an interesting riddle for young children. Check to see if children notice the absurdities in it. Invite the children to come up with more answers for the man. If they need prompting, ask for the craziest thing that might grow in the sea or in the woods.

✴ Paint pictures of strawberries growing in the sea and herrings in the wood along with all of the students' own silly ideas.

THE MAN IN THE PAPER BAG

There was a man, he went mad,
He jumped into a paper bag;
The paper bag was too narrow,
He jumped into a wheelbarrow;
The wheelbarrow took on fire,
He jumped into a cow byre;
The cow byre was too nasty,
He jumped into an apple pasty;
The apple pasty was too sweet,
He jumped into Chester-le-Street;
Chester-le-Street was full of stones,
He fell down and broke his bones.

☆Activities☆

✳ This was used as an old British skipping rhyme, but the silliness works for any occasion! And believe it or not, young children love the morbid quality of a rhyme like this. It gives children a chance to say scary things in a safe, playful way.

✳ What other things could happen to the poor old man? Children love to think of and say the grossest things, so let them! What would be the grossest things that could happen in this rhyme? Add it in and say it again!

THE COUNTESS OF DIDDLEDEE DEEZ

By Deb Hensley

The countess of Diddledee Deez
Played pinochle under the trees.
She drank buttermilk
While the inch worms made silk
And her underwear blew on the line in the breeze,
And her underwear blew in the breeze!

☆Activities☆

* This is a good rhyme to chant as children are "washing" the doll
  clothes. String a clothes line across the classroom at children's height
  and provide clothespins for them to use. Encourage students to hang
  the clothes in patterns: by color, size, etc.

* Explain that pinochle is a card game that grown-ups sometimes play.
  Ask: What card games do you like to play? Then get a few decks of
  cards for children to use at play time. Some children's card games, like
  Concentration and Go Fish, are excellent skill builders.

Creating Your Own Rhymes With Children

As you will discover when you teach the rhymes in this collection, children love to play with words! So why not create some chants and rhymes of your own? Creating nonsense rhymes, silly chants, simple poems, and songs with young children is a truly exciting way for them to explore the meaning of words. It is this kind of free-form word play that gives them a context for the concepts they are beginning to form, and allows them to be creative and comfortable with language on their terms.

The process of creating nonsense rhymes with children can be quite simple or very complex, depending on how far adults and kids want to go. Rhymes and chants can be created in the car on the way to preschool, in the classroom while waiting in line, or during meal time! They can start as simply as inviting a child to find one word that rhymes with another (FAT CAT) and then progress into a rhyme game where together you see how many rhyming words can fit into a sentence: The FAT CAT SAT on the BASEBALL BAT as she swatted at a GNAT with her big FLAT HAT! (Of course, adults can help supply those encouraging connecting words if necessary!)

Helping a child through the creative process as she discovers the way words sound is the first step in a good language experience. Simple word games can progress into rhymes and stories. Keep in mind these concepts as you and your students play with words together:

1. Repeat: As you and the child are beginning to play with words, simply repeat what you hear her say. Try repeating in a whisper, then in a high voice, then in a low voice. See how many different ways you can accent syllables together: EL-e-phant, el-e-PHANT. el-e-phant. This invites a child to view the word from many different angles and to discover that an elephant is still an elephant, no matter how you say it!

2. Vary: Children are masters at coming up with new twists on language. Youngsters' ideas of how to express themselves will often surprise and take you down new language roads. Don't be afraid to follow! You can jump in with your own ideas, too!. Start nonsense rhymes with children by varying the first letter of a word until the children get the idea of how sounds match: Monkey, Nunkey, Stunky, Blunky! Take turns making rhymes for words—even (or perhaps ESPECIALLY) when they don't mean anything!

3. Connect: When children seem ready, start connecting the fun word rhymes you have been creating in poems or stories. Sometimes children will do this completely on their own and your job will simply be to express delight. However, you may encourage students to link rhyming words by getting them started with simple nonsensical stories. Don't try to make the stories overly sweet or cute. You'll find that children love wacky humor; in fact, the sillier and more absurd, the better! Here's an example:

> *Martha the MONKEY was a kindergarten FLUNKY*
> *She tied up all the BLUNKY and dumped it in the JUNKY!*

4. Reflect: At this point in the process, invite children to think about the *meaning* of words. With the rhyming experience they've accumulated, children should be able to create silly chants that actually hang together a little bit. One way to get started is to use the concepts of "same" and "different." For example, ask: How is a camel like a table? How are your glasses like a picture? How is a bird like money? How are eyes like a light bulb? You might create a chant with children that incorporates some of these ideas:

> *My camel has four legs just like the table in the hall.*
> *My glasses have a frame just like the picture on the wall.*
> *My birdie has a bill just like the money in your pocket.*
> *My eyes can light right up just like a light bulb in a socket!*

5. Surprise! The element of surprise is essential when creating rhymes and poems with children. For example, you might take a very familiar rhyme or chant and change the words:

> *This little piggy went to the beach.*
> *This little piggy stayed home and played Monopoly.*
> *This little piggy had peanut butter and pickle sandwiches.*
> *This little piggy had prunes.*
> *This little piggy cried, "This is way cool, man!" all the way home.*

You might want to write down the rhymes you create as children dictate their thoughts to you. Children might even choose to illustrate their rhymes and chants with paints, collages, or photos and bind them into a book. However the process evolves, the most important thing is to let children take the lead. You can always encourage them with new ideas, but letting children take control when playing with words will sustain their interest and empower them to keep going. Have fun!

**"Education has not to do with filling a pail,
but rather the lighting a flame."
—Heraclitus**